DEVELOPMENT APPRAISAL OF LAND IN HONG KONG

Development Appraisal of Land in Hong Kong

LI LING-HIN

The Chinese University Press

ISBN 962-201-776-2

THE CHINESE UNIVERSITY PRESS
The Chinese University of Hong Kong
SHA TIN, N.T., HONG KONG
Fax: +852 2603 6692
+852 2603 7355
E-mail: cup@cuhk.edu.hk
Web-site: http://www.cuhk.edu.hk/cupress/w1.htm

Printed in Hong Kong

To Vivienne, My Dearest Wife

Contents

Figures and Tables

Figures

Tables

Preface

"When you possess land, you possess wealth." This is an old Chinese wisdom. In Hong Kong, this is even the motto for most young ambitious people. While most people understand the importance of the land market to the overall economy in Hong Kong, not too many academic studies have been attempted to explain the overall mechanism of the land market. Real estate market has always been a major wealth-generating source not only for major developers, but also for ordinary flat-owners. With a large population and relatively strong economy, demand for both domestic and commercial properties is bound to be consistently strong in this economy. As demand for land is a derived demand, this in turn pushes demand for land to a consistently high level. While most people in the real estate business would argue against the application of more sophisticated development appraisal models by saying that the Hong Kong land market is too small to justify the effort, one should always remember that real estate after all is a business. Like all other businesses, land development is about cash flow. When carrying out development feasibility study in the land market, if investors would like to take a much longer term perspective, a proper appraisal should be conducted which will not only provide the answer of the maximum price the investor should pay for the site, but also the possible changes in cash flow during the course of development.

When we talk about development appraisal of land, we tend to put too much emphasis on the valuation of the most probable price we should pay for the site. But very often will we find that land price is only the first stage of cash flow in the development process. What developers and investors are generally concerned with, is the changes that may occur during the development process. This is the major reason why I have been trying to use discounted cash flow (D.C.F.) in most of the examples in this book. I should emphasize here that the D.C.F. models used here are very much standardized and readers should be able to find out that the flexibility allowed in the D.C.F. model is ready to take any variations that would fit into the investors own circumstances.

Having said all these, one should also bear in mind that the major criticism of the cash flow model is the problems of making all the assumptions. To this, I would like to point out that the application of the cash flow model in a development project is more feasible than just an investment appraisal as the development period is normally shorter than the life of a commercial building. Hence, forecasting to this extent is more reliable in a development appraisal, given the right data base. The fact that no one can forecast with a hundred percent accuracy for what will happen tomorrow is no excuse for not doing this at all. This is just like the fact that the land market here will not remain as efficient as the past forever.

What this book tries to suggest is a cash flow development appraisal model, which has been known in the real estate industry for a long time, that be used in a development process not only for valuation purpose but also a financial planning. The cash flow model used in this book does not intend to be considered to be "the" best solution to development appraisal. As with other traditional valuation approaches, there are bound to be some technical problems associated with it. However, if it can provide us with some other angle to look at real estate development, it is worth examining the possibility of application in our market. I have never been encouraged by the common excuse that since everybody in the business is employing the traditional methods of appraisal, there is no need for improvement and change. If we pay some attention to the things happening around us, we will notice that there is always call for improvement and change everyday. The ideas raised in this book will hopefully steer land development appraisal in the market towards more investment-based rather than speculation-based.

L. H. Li
June, 1997
The University of Hong Kong

Acknowledgement

I would like to express my deepest gratitude to all the supporting staff in the Department of Real Estate and Construction for their support and help in all sort of clerical functions, not only for me but also other teaching staff. Thanks should also be given to Keith McKinnell, Head of the Department as well as other academic staff for their support in research in the department. I am also grateful to Jimmy Louey, Edward Mak and Rex Yip for their technical information concerning the land management system in Hong Kong. As usual, I am indebted to my parents for their support in my choice of career which gives me a great motivation to work hard. Finally, I would like to thank my wife, Vivienne, for her love, and unconditional support and appreciation of my work.

Chapter 1

Introduction

In 1975, P. J. Roberts wrote a book about the valuation of development land in Hong Kong. This was the first attempt to relate valuation or appraisal principles of real estate to Hong Kong. In the past 20 years, the land market in Hong Kong boomed to the extent that substantial revenue comes to the government from the sale of land and property and related taxes (Walker, Chau and Lai, 1995). In addition, the reform of the urban land market in China also to a great extent models the Hong Kong land management system (Li, 1996). At the same time, appraisal theories internationally have been refined and improved with the advent of high speed computers. Nevertheless, in the 20 years since Roberts' book, no major academic publication has attempted to fill the gap of relating appraisal principles to land and real estate development in Hong Kong. For Hong Kong land has always been a valuable source of income generation for investors and the government. Appraisal of land development is instrumental to a developing and even a well-developed land market as it increases the efficiency of the market mechanism. The attempt of this book is to facilitate the flourishing land market in Hong Kong by introducing a theoretical framework of investment and development appraisal for academic reference.

Land is different from other tradable commodities in the broadest sense that it does not have a production cost function in the way steel or an apartment does. In this way, we cannot easily appraise the value of land without some theoretical framework as the foundation. Therefore, there is a need to discuss the theoretical definition of land value before we go into details of the discussion of the development appraisal models.

Having discussed the origin of land value, we shall start looking at the land market in Hong Kong. We shall examine briefly land market activities in Hong Kong in the past 10 years and their relationship with the property market and the economy as a whole. In addition, we shall also look at the new comer in the Hong Kong land market, the investment from mainland China during Hong Kong's transition into part of China's economy.

Following this, we shall turn to the examination of the implications of development controls on developers and the ways by which a developer/land owner can apply to the government for the modifications of these controls. In Hong Kong, since the government owns all the land, it will have power to impose certain conditions and restrictions on the use of land whenever land is being auctioned. In addition, such conditions and restrictions may be carried forward in subsequent transactions of land. Hence a landowner or prospective purchaser of land may want to apply for modification of these conditions so that redevelopment can take place more profitably. All these considerations are linked to a central issue of this book: how do we appraise the development value of land? In the subsequent chapters, the various appraisal models will be explained and examined.

The first discussion centres on the introduction of the real estate appraisal models. Value of real estate may vary according to the different needs of appraisal and the types of property we are looking at. There are basically five major methods for the appraisal of real estate values. The first one is the most common way of market comparison. The other methods include the approximation of value by cost in the cost approach and the estimation of rental value by the profit method. The application of these models depends on the market situation and availability of information. In addition, the two most technical models, namely the investment method and the residual valuation model will be discussed in detail as they relate to development appraisal more readily than others.

As a conclusion, we state in the final part of the book that development appraisal is fundamental to developers especially in a market where information is not adequate and the structure of the market is not as well-developed as others. In such cases, a well-structured development appraisal will not only help the developer to assess the value of land but also force the developer to examine the various components in the development process more carefully. Appraisal should be given more credit in land development not only for its function of providing a numerical figure of possible land price to be realized at government auction, but also for its analytical capacity for the developer/investor in the changing environment. Where it is possible, scientific models on forecasting should be incorporated into the appraisal one so that the results of the development appraisal will be more robust and reliable.

LAND PRICE AND LAND VALUE

Land value is a theoretical concept whose nature is basically the same in any economy as long as a market mechanism is set up and allowed to operate for the allocation of land. Land price, however, can be "controlled," especially in a socialist economy. It is therefore essential to examine the theoretical relationship between price and value and the appraisal process through which value can be assessed and turned into a reference point for price.

Land price is always a historical figure. It is only created after a market transaction has taken place. Value on the other hand has a future implication. It shows how the property asset will benefit the owner in the future holding period in both utility and monetary terms. Under this concept, the measure of future possible income from land is more appropriate in explaining the value element.

It may be argued that a property owner is only interested in the probable selling price. If the market is accepting a certain price level as the clearing price, the personal subjective level of utility of an individual investor does not matter. Fraser (1988) elaborates this argument by making an analogy with the stock market that:

> ... if a client wishes to know the market value of his shares, the broker will not undertake any analysis, but will call up the appropriate page on computer screen showing current price....

However, this analogy can also be utilized to emphasize the

importance of finding value first as a reference point for estimating possible selling price. In analysing the potential of a particular share in the stock market, one will always need to look at the potential of the company. This will require an analysis of the management style of the existing board of directors and senior management, past records of the performance of the company as well as the announced investment plans of the company. These details cannot be revealed by looking at the current trading price on the computer. If investment is the objective of the whole exercise, then there is definitely a need to find the investment "value" of the share and compare it with the current trading price of the share of the company. Hence, finding value is also the first and necessary step for setting the appropriate price level.

Valuation or appraisal is not about the mathematical process through which a statistically precise figure can be created and proved. It is about the explanation of the interrelationship between the different variables in the real estate market from the micro level and in the economy from the macro level. Without such an understanding, the application of appraisal models is very restrictive. Brown (1991) remarks that:

> ... the correct role of valuation models is to define the economic relationship between the relevant variables in order to arrive at values which could establish a market in equilibrium.... The principle function of valuation models in this context therefore is to establish whether individual properties offered for sale are either under- or over-priced relative to their equilibrium market values ... valuation is drafted in terms of expectations and is a reflection on the quality and the amount of information....

Land price and land value can be substantially different for the former depends very much on the market atmosphere at the point of time when the particular piece of land is being negotiated for transaction, whereas the latter points to a more subjective measure of total future returns that can be obtained from the ownership of land. Ordinary commodities always have a price before they enter into exchange. For instance, we can always be sure about the price of a box of chocolates once we walk into a supermarket without having first to negotiate with the cashier. Prices for most commodities exist before the commodities enter into the exchange mechanism. In the case of land, it is very different.

Appraisal is a process which determines the value of the commodity. If there is an exchange mechanism available for the commodity, then appraisal is the process of assessing value for ascertaining the most probable price in the market. It is very difficult for appraisal models to determine market price unless everybody in the market has the same value-judgement. The most obvious example is commodity with a high personal value such as old (not antique) furniture passing from previous generations. The furniture itself may be "valued" highly by the present owner as it carries a family history. But market price for it may approach zero given its functional use value.

It may be true to say value itself does not necessarily depend on the "market mechanism" because value does not depend on the existence of exchange in the market and it exists before the necessity for the commodity to enter the market. But its measurement will certainly depend on the market mechanism if the purpose of measurement is a standardized and objective comparison with other parties in the market for the purpose of exchange.

Since the concept of value can vary with different commodities, the distinction made by the property profession becomes more specific to the definition of the value of real estate. Albritton (1982) concludes that:

> The monetary sum paid for real property is customarily reported as price and represents a fact. Conversely, value is always expressed as an opinion or estimate.... Value is basically a relationship between a person and the object desired.... Value may be defined generally as the estimated present worth of future benefits.... Sale price reflects the value relationship established between a buyer and a seller for a property on a specific date. It can hardly be argued that price conclusively establishes value if the market reflects sales of other, similar properties at different prices at approximately the same date.... (p. 17)

Price is therefore a result of market activities, or specifically, the result of market negotiations that have been going on before a contract price is finally agreed. Price is time specific and dependent on the factors appearing at that point of time during the negotiation and transaction. Value represents a longer term perspective. It is a dynamic measurement rather than a static figure of the worthiness of an object to an owner or potential owner. In Chinese-speaking societies such as Hong Kong, Taiwan and mainland China, it is always confusing when the term "appraisal" is translated into "price guessing" or *gujia* rather than the ascertainment of value.

In terms of this intermingled relationship between price and value, Lichtenstein (1983) explains much more concisely that:

> ... value originates in production; money price originates in circulation. The connection between value and money price is therefore the connection between the spheres of production and circulation ... values determine direct prices; direct prices get transformed into prices of production; and market prices will fluctuate around these prices of production ... while this process of successive price transformation takes place, the value structure of output stays the same, the prices at which this mass of value circulates throughout the system do not, and cannot, alter the value of this mass....

Patrick Corcoran (1987) explains a similar situation in the States where there are both rising vacancy rates and acquisition prices. He analyses the market from two separate but related economic perspectives, i.e. within the classical theory of investment in capital goods, real estate, as one factor of production; and within the portfolio theory. The whole research framework stresses the linkage and interaction between the rental market for real estate and the asset market. He concludes that:

> .... This two market viewpoint is essential for an understanding of real estate development. We have focused on the 1980s in this article, but the linkage between asset and rental markets is helpful in understanding both the past and the future....

He explains the fact that there could be an increase in asset demand without corresponding increase in the rental market. This increase results from the lowering of the user cost which is triggered by the decrease of interest rates as well as inflation.

His research provides another aspect of analysing property values, i.e. the value of property depends on a set of variables, the interrelationship of which controls the movement of both the rental and capital values. Analysis, and hence appraisal, of property values needs a deeper understanding of the economic system within which the real estate market operates. The appraisal process is only one part of the economic process. Any meaningful appraisal model or process should therefore be able to explain the meaning and interrelationship between all the variables, besides giving the final numerical figure.

Appraisal is the process of establishing the value of land before it is exchanged. Depending on the current market situation, further adjustments (either upward or downward) are made to this value which becomes the price when the demand and supply sides come to a conclusion. Appraisal should not therefore aim at finding price, although the concluded selling price does feed back into future appraisal process in the ascertaining of value.

Why is this distinction so important? The answer is the peculiarity of land as a tradable commodity in the market. For ordinary commodities, such as oranges, value can be examined from two perspectives, subjective and objective. The subjective way normally refers to the utility derived from having the commodity. The utility of having an orange may vary from individual to individual, just as it does with land. However, this variation of utility will not be exhibited in the price of an individual orange. Hence, one particular orange does not normally generate substantially more utility than any other orange, but this is the case with land. There is always a locational difference between different plots of land so that there is prime site and secondary site for different uses.

The objective perspective of value can be explained by looking at production costs. Under such criteria, oranges will have a fairly uniform value basis because production cost will be more or less the same within the same plantation area. What makes the difference is probably the profit margin. But as long as the market is relatively competitive, this profit margin will also tend to smooth out, at least within a certain neighbourhood. This, however, does not apply to land.

First of all, there is no production cost for land, except for site improvement costs. This makes it more difficult to have an objective basis for land in ascertaining value, except in an indirect way by looking at the product on the land. Secondly, different individual pieces of land may produce different values of product. Hence, for oranges, it is how much is spent on producing it, while for land, it is how much can be made by utilizing it.

Sheppard and Barnes (1990) give a political economic view on the distinction between those commodities which go through production and those which do not:

> ... the prices (rents) of land and natural resources in the political economic approach are unlike other commodity prices. For the general system of production prices in a political economic perspective based on reproduction costs; one where price levels of produced goods are set so that they cover the costs of production (input costs, wages and profits), thereby enabling the commodity to be reproduced in the future. With non-produced goods such as natural resources, however, there are no reproduction costs ... then two questions arise. First, what determines rental levels? (rents cannot be equal to costs of production because there are none). Second, and more fundamentally why should natural resources receive a rent at all? (If there are no reproduction costs there is seemingly no justification for levying a price)....

The quantification of value will therefore help estimate the most probable price achievable in the market. With the attachment of monetary quantities to value, value and price are drawn together. O'Keefe (1974) confirms this from a legal point of view in that in a capitalist economy:

> ... money is also the matrix, the medium in which value is developed, the formative part of value, the mould into which value is cast.... The use of money implies scarcity which is an attribute of land, so that land transaction involves the exchange of one scarce thing for another....

Price can be an exemplification of value provided some conditions are fulfilled. According to Sinden and Worell (1979), the first step in using market prices is to determine whether they are truly competitive,

> .... A competitive market must have freedom of exchange and many sellers and buyers. The prices themselves must meet two other tests. First, they must measure the opportunity cost of the marginal unit exchanged and thus the social cost of that unit. Second, they must equate supply and demand. An acceptable price measures the willingness of those involved to exchange the marginal unit....

This is an ideal situation. The real estate market is rarely truly competitive and perfect. Information is rarely available to all players in the market for the same costs. Hence, assessment of value first for the estimation of the most probable market price is even more important.

THE ORIGIN OF LAND VALUE

Having established the importance of assessing land value as the first step in the appraisal process, we need to understand what exactly constitutes land value. As mentioned before, land itself has no cost in the broadest sense. Land value arises because of the differential profitability that can be realized from using land for a particular type of economic activity. Land value in fact is realized in the form of land rent which has an extensive foundation in the field of political economy. In order for this book not to be involved in the enormous and interesting subject of political economy, a very brief analysis of land rent based on the general principles laid down by Ricardo (1963) will be explained first. Accordingly, assume we are still living in the Stone Age when the economic system is very very primitive, land areas available for development far exceed the number of land users. Land users are basically free to choose wherever they want to develop without having to pay for the use of land. Under this economic environment, agriculture is the only feasible land development. In this case, people will quite normally choose to go the most fertile and accessible land to carry out economic activities, so long as they are safe from being attacked by dinosaurs.

Assuming potato is the only plant being planted and traded in the market, the price of potatoes in the market is determined by the production function of planting potatoes. As the economy becomes more mature with a growing population, demand for potatoes grows as well. At this point, more people will join the business of growing potatoes. Here a sequence of events will occur. First of all, with a growing number of land users demanding to use land, the political structure of the economy will change so that a group of people, with their special political or physical power will secure the ownership of the most fertile land (we may call it class one land). Secondly, with the growing number of land users, the most fertile land for growing potatoes will become saturated. Given the steady growth in demand for potatoes, latecomers to this potato-growing industry will have to search for other land to start their businesses.

Naturally, these latecomers will go to the less fertile land (we may say class two land) for the production of potatoes. However, as these class two sites are less productive, land users will have to spend more on the improvement of the land such as adding fertilizers, etc. At this point, production function of potatoes on class two land will be increased. As we learn from above that market price of potatoes is determined by the production function, the overall market price will rise by the increase of production cost on class two land. Further assume that the demand for potatoes is inelastic, the rise in market price of potatoes will not deter a shrink of demand. In this case, land users on class one land will enjoy a supernormal profit due to the rise in price.

However, because of the established land-ownership system, this supernormal profit on class one land will have to go to the landlord as land rent. This is because if the land users refuse to pay this sum, the landlord can relinquish the land user's occupation right and replace him by another user on class two land who would feel no difference whether producing on class one site with payment of rent or remaining where he is.

However, as far as class two sites are concerned, so long as that land is not saturated, it remains free to the users. As a result, if we project this behaviour, land rent will be determined by the differential productivity of various types of land in the economy. Now, let us go back to the future from the Stone Age. In a modern urban economy, the economic activities on urban land will invariably be real estate development. If we substitute this urban economy into the simple framework established above, the potatoes above become properties on land in a modern economy. Hence, in an urban economy, land rent is determined by the price differential between properties. This is an important concept as in the later part of this book we will introduce the fundamental nature of land value, i.e. the residual nature of land value.

The residual nature of land value also brings out an important concept in the property market. This is that, in the normal situation, land price is determined by how much a developer can expect from the completed development. From the total revenue, a developer would then deduct the construction expenses and his own remuneration for taking on this risky project. Whatever is left, or the residual element, belongs to the price for land. Hence, it is not logical to assume that land price contributes to rising property price, but, rather, that high demand for property leads to high property prices. This in turn leads to higher affordability on the part of developer to bid for land, as the residual element in the development now becomes higher. In this way of thinking, the normal contention that land price pushes property price to a record high may not be sustained. This will be discussed further in the later chapter on development appraisal of land.

Before tackling the core subject of appraisal models, let us look at the structure and performance of the Hong Kong land market as well as at the various constraints put on this market.

Chapter 2

The Land Market in Hong Kong

THE LAND MANAGEMENT SYSTEM IN HONG KONG

Historical Background

When Hong Kong Island (not including Kowloon Peninsula) was first ceded to the British in 1842 under the Treaty of Nanking (Nanjing), it was a fishing village — nothing more than a barren rock. The British government at that time wanted Hong Kong as an entrepôt and a safe place for their ships which were carrying out trading activities in the region. The importance of Hong Kong grew as the economy developed, and by the First and Second Treaties of Peking (Beijing), in 1860 and 1898 respectively, Kowloon and the New Territories were leased to the British government.

LAND TENURE SYSTEM IN HONG KONG

The present land tenure system used in Hong Kong is closely related to her history. *Leasehold system*, which allows for absolute perpetual title of land to be vested in the government as owner of all land, was used as a method of disposing of government land soon after Hong Kong became a British Colony in 1842. Except for the site of St. Johns Cathedral, all land in Hong Kong is held under formal Crown leases for a term of years absolute.

Mode of Conveyance of Public Land

Public auction, *tender*, and *private treaty grant* are the three basic methods of disposal of land in most economies. The Hong Kong government's basic policy is to sell government land leases to the highest bidder at the public auction. The successful bidder becomes the lessee of government land. The terms of the auction are contained in the "Particulars and Conditions of Sale" which is regarded as an agreement for lease. In this document, there are basically two major parts. The first part is general conditions which include conditions on reserve price; completion of sale; payment of premium; disclosure of principal and rateable value. The second part of this document contains more specific conditions on the development of land. These include building covenants; use of land; master layout plan and landscape proposals; building regulations; town planning regulations, total floor area allowed on the site and maximum site coverage; conditions on design, disposition and height; carpark layout as well as vehicular access. In addition, there is always a survey sheet showing the location of the site. Upon compliance with the terms and conditions as set out in the Conditions of Sale, a Certificate of Compliance will be issued by the relevant District Land Officer conferring upon the Crown lease.

Some land is not sold by public auction but by tender. This is mainly land where the user is strictly defined and the sale is unlikely to attract general interest, or where government wishes to examine in advance detailed proposals for the development of a particular lot. Land for community purposes such as public housing, the Home Ownership Scheme, public utilities, schools, churches, clinics, welfare, and certain charitable purposes is usually granted by private treaty grant.

The sale of leases either by public auction or tender is generally referred to as land sales in Hong Kong. This is different from the selling of land under a freehold system. It is the sale of the land lease but not the land. Therefore, an owner of a piece of land in Hong Kong does not actually own it, but has the exclusive right to possess the same for a definite period of time.

There is another way of conveying land in Hong Kong before July, 1997, which is locally referred to as Letter "A" and Letter "B." Letter "A" and Letter "B" are those land exchange entitlements issued by the Hong Kong government from 1960 to 1983 as a large-scale rural redevelopment plan. This system arose as indigenous villagers in the New Territories were not pre-pared to give up their entire holdings of ancestral land for an award of cash compensation alone. They wished to be compen-sated with an alternative piece of land. Therefore, when the government began to acquire land in the New Territories, the Letters "A" and "B" system was introduced to give promises to provide land for development in return for the surrender of ancestral land prior to its reversion under the Crown Lands Resumption Ordinance.

Until March 1983, no more Letters "A" and "B" for land resumption were issued and the monetarization of the Letters "A" and "B" was introduced. Many real estate developers obtain land from the indigenous landowners by purchasing their ex-change documents. To cite an example, the four developers in Hong Kong, namely Sun Hung Kai Properties, Nam Fung Development, Henderson Land Development and Chinachem Group hold the certificates that could be exchanged for a total of about 1.3 million square feet of agricultural land.

Terms of Land Leases

As parts of Hong Kong were ceded and leased in different periods in her history, land tenure systems, particularly the leasing period and renewability of the lease, vary slightly between Hong Kong Island, Kowloon and the New Territories. The term of the leases varies from 999 years, to 99 years, to 75 years and the lease can be renewable or non-renewable. Attached to each lease is a set of lease conditions which stipulate the time period, renewability and permitted development of the land.

The return of Hong Kong to Chinese rule in 1997 heralds a new phase in Hong Kong's history, but the intentions are for its system of land holding to remain largely unchanged. The Sino-British Joint Declaration sets out in Annex III that the present leasehold system will be continued and arrangements for the leasing of land will resemble the current practice in Hong Kong (see Appendix 2). The Crown Leases will be known as Govern-ment Leases.

Terms of existing leases extending beyond 1997 will be honoured, and those which will expire before 1997 might be extended to 2047 without charging any additional premium. After 1997, holders of renewal leases or new leases granted after the Declaration will have to pay an annual rent of 3% of the rateable value of their properties.

The present Hong Kong government can issue new leases with term lasting till 2047 through the existing land disposal system of public auction, tender or private treaty grant. However, in order to prevent the Hong Kong government from selling off all the land, leaving Hong Kong's future Special Administrative Region (SAR) government without a major source of revenue, it is stipulated that no more than 50 hectares of land (excluding land to be granted to Hong Kong Housing Authority for public rental housing) can be leased by the Hong Kong government in a single year during the transition period, although this limit has always been exceeded due to strong demand for residential units.

Payment for Land

There are two main types of payments for land:

1. Premium: In order to obtain a Crown Lease, the lessee pays a premium in a lump sum on the date of the lease. This is in actual fact the market land price.
2. Crown Rent: Normally a nominal sum which bears little or no relationship to the actual value of the land, it is only a legal symbol to maintain the lessor and the lessee relationship.

Resumption of Possession of Land

The Hong Kong government is empowered by certain statutes to resume procession of land for public purposes. But in such cases, the lessee has a right to claim compensation for the dispossession of land. "Public purposes" is widely defined in the Crown Lands Resumption Ordinance to include any purpose that the government may decide to be a public purpose, and the Land Development Corporation is entrusted with the task of facilitating renewal of urban areas and to advise the government as to the exercise of its power to resume land under the ordinance when an agreement to pursue the same redevelopment purpose has failed.

In the old urban areas where there is less financial incentive for redevelopment and ownership is fragmented, a large number of old buildings still remain. Many of these buildings are in poor physical condition and are situated in areas where community facilities are inadequate and road layouts are below current standards. This has called for more pro-active urban renewal actions. Urban renewal development would provide the best use of land for community needs, so as to improve the living environment and build a better city in Hong Kong. Also, through urban renewal projects, there should be a commitment that no residents would be rendered homeless.

GOVERNMENT DEPARTMENTS IN THE PLANNING, ENVIRONMENT AND LANDS BRANCH

Lands Department

- Responsible for the disposal of government land.
- In charge of land management which covers control of government land to prevent illegal occupation, and enforcement of the lease provisions should there be noncompliance with the lease conditions for the private land.
- Carries out valuation for government land transactions and variation of lease conditions.

Buildings Department

- Controls all building development on private land and ensures that standards laid down in the Buildings Ordinance are upheld.
- Ensures compliance with statutory standards of safety, health and environment in private buildings and building works.

Planning Department

- Responsible for formulating, monitoring and reviewing

Figure 1 Central Government Structure concerning Land Development

Secretariat for Planning, Environmental and Lands (SPEL) Branch

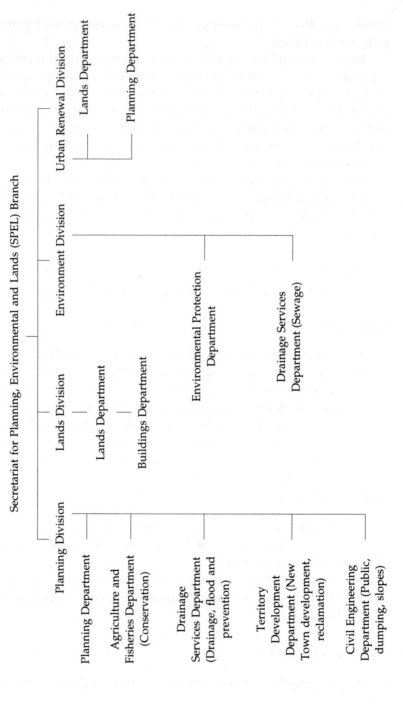

urban, rural and marine-related planning and associated programmes to provide a framework for the physical development of Hong Kong.

- Deals with all types of planning at the territorial, sub-regional and district levels.

Figure 2 Government Structure within the SPEL Branch

Lands and Planning Division

Resource Management Unit	Lands Unit
• General revenue accounts/ annual estimates	• Land policy, legislation and administration
• Recurrent resource allocations	• Buildings policy and legislation
• Finance Committee Agenda Items, Establishment Sub-Committee, Public Works Sub-Committee and Departmental Establishment Committee submissions	• Land Development Corporation matters
	• Land Commission matters
	• Potentially hazardous installations
	• Compensation for resumption and clearance
• Performance review of the PEL group of departments	• Land and Building Advisory Committee matters
• Value for money studies	

THE LAND MARKET IN HONG KONG

In Hong Kong, revenue from public land sales constitutes major income for the government. Such a phenomenon attributes to a great extent to the land tenure system in this city. While land is being auctioned periodically by the government, land owner-ship remains in the hands of the government. What is being auctioned in the City Hall is in fact the long leasehold interest (usually 999 years lease in the past). Hence, apart from the land price that a developer has to pay, he will also have to pay a nominal amount of land rent per year. This situation changes a little since the signing of the Sino-British Agreement in 1984. Accordingly all the leasehold interests auctioned since then can only last for 50 years plus the period between the auction date and 30 June 1997 (Annex III, Joint Sino-British Declaration on

Figure 3 Simplified Development (Construction) Process in HK

Demolition Consent (if any)

↓

Seek approval of general building plans from Buildings Dept.

↓

Seek approval of piling/foundation plan

↓

Approval of foundation consent obtained — consent to commence work

↓

Seek approval of structure, superstructure and drainage plans

↓

BA 14 form to report completion of foundation

↓

Apply for consent for commencement of superstructures

↓

Seek sale consent from Lands Dept. →

↓

Seek Fire Dept. Approval

↓

Apply by BA 13 form for Occupation Permit (OP)

↓

Apply for Certificate of Compliance (CC) from Lands Dept.

the Future of Hong Kong). In addition, a land premium will have to be paid which is equal to 3% of the rateable value of the land for leases ending after year 1997. Nevertheless, this does not make the land market any less interesting to the developer.

Generally speaking, the government will sell land in one of the three ways: public auction, tender and private treaty grant. Most of the land is sold through public auction for it will normally attract most of the interested developers and the competitive atmosphere in the auction venue is such that it will generate the highest land price. However, sometimes for some particular reasons, the government may not want to sell the land to the highest bidder. Such circumstances arise when the government wants to introduce competition into the industry which the particular piece of land is going to cater for, such as a container terminal operation. Government may then tend to use tender procedures in selling the land since there is no obligation for the government to accept the highest bid and the government can always invite selected candidates to submit their tenders.

Table 1 shows the areas of land and floor space sold for different uses from 1984 to 1996 (3rd quarter). We may notice from Figures 4 and 5 that the area of land sold for residential

Table 1 Land Sale Analysis (1984–1996)

Year	Use	Land Area (Sq.ft.)	GFA* (Sq.ft.)
1984	Residential	135,173	
	Industrial/Godown	425,530	
	Non-industrial	347,222	
	Commercial (+Carpark)	—	
	Total	**907,925**	
1985	Residential	824,955	
	Industrial/Godown	218,123	
	Non-industrial	259,143	
	Commercial (+Carpark)	36,909	
	Total	**1,339,130**	
1986	Residential	303,553	
	Industrial/Godown	279,754	
	Non-industrial	220,637	
	Commercial (+Carpark)	16,361	
	Total	**820,305**	
1987	Residential	451,471	
	Industrial/Godown	600,562	
	Non-industrial	28,978	
	Commercial (+Carpark)	—	
	Total	**1,081,011**	
1988	Residential	315,199	786,041
	Industrial/Godown	324,006	2,396,411
	Non-industrial	97,340	993,639
	Commercial (+Carpark)	—	—
	Total	**736,545**	**4,176,091**
1989	Residential	947,865	2,495,846
	Industrial/Godown	383,404	2,996,723
	Non-industrial	345,821	4,171,821
	Commercial (+Carpark)	—	—
	Total	**1,677,090**	**9,664,390**

Table 1 (Cont'd)

Year	Use	Land Area (Sq.ft.)	GFA (Sq.ft.)
1990	Residential	644,006	1,872,836
	Industrial/Godown	213,244	1,990,467
	Non-industrial	—	—
	Commercial (+Carpark)	181,942	1,994,834
	Total	**1,039,192**	**5,858,137**
1991	Residential	920,960	2,824,270
	Industrial/Godown	465,859	2,876,004
	Non-industrial	245,064	1,854,615
	Commercial (+Carpark)	—	—
	Total	**1,631,883**	**7,554,889**
1992	Residential	1,251,951	2,532,340
	Industrial/Godown	505,279	3,329,279
	Non-industrial	155,890	1,457,757
	Commercial (+Carpark)	—	—
	Total	**1,913,120**	**7,319,376**
1993	Residential	1,199,808	3,460,861
	Industrial/Godown	344,803	2,078,684
	Non-industrial	162,504	1,413,660
	Commercial (+Carpark)	222,384	1,256,060
	Total	**1,929,499**	**8,209,265**
1994	Residential	550,464	1,642,540
	Industrial/Godown	276,281	1,552,946
	Non-industrial	122,461	1,246,805
	Commercial (+Carpark)	287,070	1,526,605
	Total	**1,236,276**	**5,968,896**
1995	Residential	1,522,890	3,071,075
	Industrial/Godown	573,439	2,904,917.9
	Non-industrial	217,410	1,302,631.9
	Commercial (+Carpark)	111,833	1,151,948.5
	Total	**2,425,572**	**8,430,573.3**
1996	Non-industrial	254,372	2,173,660.3
(up to November)	Residential	231,082	184,716.9
	Total	**485,454**	**2,358,377.2**

Sources: Lands Department, Hong Kong Government, and various
newspaper reports.
* GFA: gross floor area.

Figure 4 Land Areas Sold in Government Land Auctions from
1988–1996 (up to November)

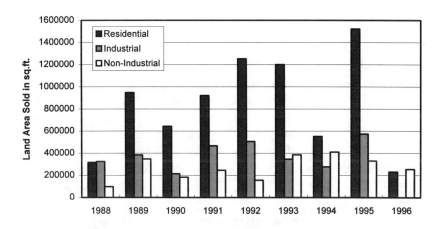

Figure 5 GFA Sold in Government Land Auctions from
1988–1996 (up to November)

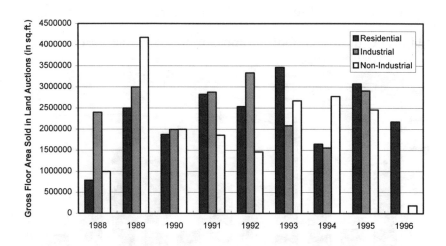

use has been increasing since the late 1980s, while the area
of land sold for industrial use has been decreasing since 1991.
This is obvious as demand for residential properties is generally
on an upward trend whereas demand for industrial land has

been shrinking recently as more and more factories move to China.

However, when we look at the actual floor space that can be developed from the land sold, we may be able to relate this to market behaviour in the last few years. From Figure 4, we notice that the residential floor area to be developed from the land sold between 1988–1990 was not consistently substantial. This may have contributed to the low supply of residential flats in 1991–1993 (as development normally takes an average of 2 to 3 years to be completed.). This in turn, could help to explain partly why residential prices jumped substantially in the same period. The supply of land for various uses is therefore a passive reaction to the changes in the property market. This, to a certain extent, may contribute to the fluctuation of price levels in the property market.

We can try to further analyse the reaction of the land market to the changes in the economic structure. Figure 6 shows the relationship between the All Manufacturing Index (reflecting the average industrial production in Hong Kong with base year set in 1986) and the yearly supply of industrial land by the government (in sq.ft.). We can see from Figure 6 that, on average,

Figure 6 Industrial Output and Supply of Industrial Land 1984–1994

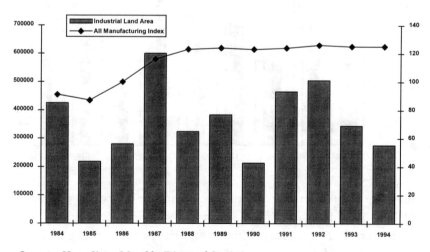

Source: *Hong Kong Monthly Digest of Statistics.*

industrial output started to stagnate from 1988 until 1994 but the supply of industrial land varied between this period with a rising trend (except 1990) until 1992 then started to shrink. This reflects how inflexible our land supply mechanism can be. This can also be shown by looking at the real changes in the price and rent of industrial premises from Figures 7, 8 and 9. Price levels (after adjustment for inflation effects) of industrial premises started to fall from 1989 until 1992, which was the period of increased supply in the land market. When supply began to shrink, the price of industrial properties began to pick up. There is certainly a time lag in the supply and demand mechanism which should be carefully looked at by the government if a more stable land market is the prime objective of the relevant authority when selling government land through the public land auction or the "public land market" mechanism.

In addition, we can also examine the importance of the "public land market" in the overall land market (total assignments of land registered in the Lands Registry) in Hong Kong. From Table 2, we can make a comparison of the values of land

Figure 7 Real Rental Index by Types of Premises for 1984–1994

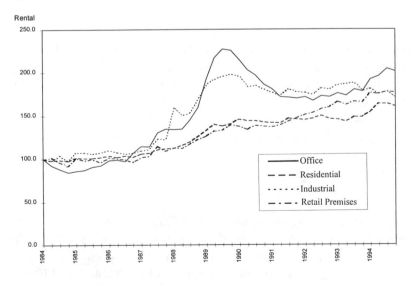

Source: Chau, Li and Webb, 1996.

Figure 8 Real Price Index by Types of Premises for 1984–1994

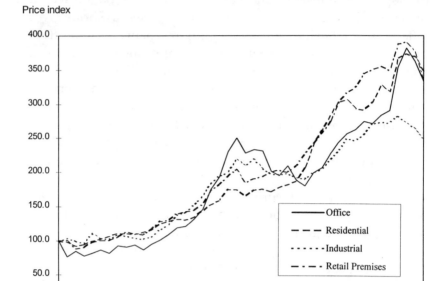

Price index

Source: Chau, Li and Webb, 1996.

realized in the public land market and in the overall land market from 1985 to 1994. We find that in terms of value, the supply mechanism through the government land auction programme is inadequate when compared to the effort the developers have put into assembling land in the private sector. This is even the case when the property market is on the rising trend such as between 1991–1994.

New Player in the Market

When Hong Kong becomes part of China, there are also some interesting phenomenon in the Hong Kong land market. The major one is the involvement of investment funds with a mainland Chinese background in land market activities. Table 3 and Figure 10 show the growing interests of these China Related Funds (CRFs)

Figure 9 Changes in Price Index (Real and Nominal) in the Industrial Market

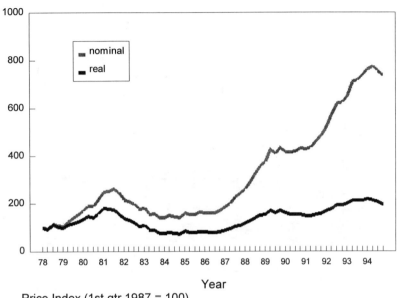

Year

Price Index (1st qtr 1987 = 100)

Source: *Hong Kong Monthly Digest of Statistics.*

Table 2 Share of the Public Land Market in the Overall Land Market 1985–1994

Year	Overall Land Market (HK$ million)	Public Land Market (HK$ million)	Share of Public Land Market in the Overall Market
1985	6,919.56	2,558.00	36.97%
1986	28,122.39	2,243.00	7.98%
1987	17,915.32	3,122.00	17.43%
1988	32,410.52	2,220.00	6.85%
1989	31,176.10	10,018.00	32.13%
1990	21,419.61	2,159.70	10.08%
1991	41,071.78	7,424.50	18.08%
1992	58,225.31	8,741.90	15.01%
1993	81,791.48	15,880.00	19.42%
1994	80,977.00	14,521.20	17.93%

Source: *Hong Kong Monthly Digest of Statistics.*

Table 3 China Related Funds (CRFs) Acquisitions in the Government Land Sales

Date	Location	Use	Area (sq.m)	CRF involved	Ownership by the CRFs	Partner
6/90	Fanling N.T.	Residential	4,841	COLI*	100.0%	
1/91	Tai Po, N.T.	Residential	12,090	COLI	30.0%	
10/91	Shatin, N.T.	Residential	21,350	COLI	12.0%	
12/91	Kowloon	Residential	6,417	COLI	30.0%	Sino Land
3/92	Yuen Long, N.T.	Residential	5,320	CITIC†	33.3%	Kerry Properties, Sino Land
4/92	Hong Kong Island	Industrial	5,538	CITIC	100.0%	
3/93	Kowloon	Commercial	20,660	CITIC	50.0%	Swire
6/93	Shatin, N.T.	Residential	15,320	COLI	25.0%	Sino Land
7/93	Yuen Long, N.T.	Residential	10,320	COLI	30.0%	Sino Land/Nam Fung
11/93	Yuen Long, N.T.	Residential	4,350	H.K. Macau	100.0%	
12/93	Kowloon	Residential	43,520	COLI	10.0%	Sino Land/Nam Fung

Source: Hastings and Li (1996).

* COLI   China Overseas Land and Investment Ltd.
† CITIC   China International Trust and Investment Corporation.

Figure 10 Involvement of CRFs in Hong Kong Land Market

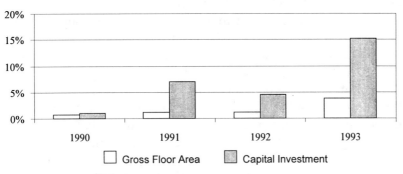

Source: Same as Table 3.

in Hong Kong's land market. One particular feature is that they have been on leaning curve about the development process in a market economy not only through active involvement but also through joint venture exercises with major local developers (Hastings and Li, 1996). In this respect, we may be able to find a much longer-term strategy in these Chinese investments than just short term speculation (a more typical example is the successful tender made by the China Inter-national Trust and Investment Company [CITIC] in the Central Business District [CBD] of Hong Kong. In order to establish their headquarters building in the heart of the CBD in Hong Kong, CITIC paid a very high price [approx. US$770/ sq.ft.] for the site which was currently occupied by the British Navy [HMS Tamar]. Coincidentally, the building next to the site will be occupied by the China's People's Liberation Army after July 1997 as their headquarters in Hong Kong).

DEVELOPMENT CONTROLS IN HONG KONG

In Hong Kong, land development is basically constrained by three types of development control, namely planning controls such as statutory control and non-statutory guidelines, outline zoning plans in the urban areas and development permission areas in rural areas; building controls as stipulated by the Building Or-dinance and Building (Planning) Regulations; and finally the lease controls laid down specifically for each individual piece of land sold. In this section, we will only be giving an introduction to lease controls and the modification of such controls through application to the relevant government bodies.

When the government intends to sell land through public auction, there will normally be a set of documents concerning the particulars and conditions of sale available for any party interested to consider the feasibility of the proposition. In this document, there are basically three main parts. The first part is the particulars of the lot which describes the registry number of the lot in the Hong Kong Lands Registry, the detailed location (with map), the approximate land area and the land rent payable per annum. For the land rent, it is normally stated as a certain sum per annum up to 30 June 1997 and thereafter an amount equal to 3% of the rateable value for the time being of the lot.

The next section goes on to the general conditions of sale. Under the general conditions, items such as the qualification of the purchaser as the highest bidder, payment of the land premium and land rent, maintenance and boundary of the site and the rights of the government when there is breach of lease conditions are explained. Under the special conditions, main items described normally include the following:

1. Building Covenant
   The purchaser shall develop the lot by erection of building(s) complying with the conditions in the lease and any other relevant ordinances and regulations. Such building(s) must be completed or made fit for occupation on or before a stipulated date in the future.

2. User Clause
   This condition specifies the purpose(s) of the building(s) to be erected on the lot such as private residential etc.

3. Master Layout Plan
   The purchaser shall within a specified period of the signing of the sale agreement submit by his authorized person (as defined in the Building Ordinance) a master layout plan for approval. Such a plan should include the formation level of the lot; the position, widths and levels of any proposed roads and pedestrian ways; the nature, height and gross floor area of the building to be erected; indication of hard and soft landscaping,

indication of car parking proposals (if any) and the stages or phases by which the purchaser proposes to develop. Once approved, the plan must be complied with unless a record of modification, amendment, variation or alteration has been deposited in the relevant land registry.

4.   Development Conditions

Such conditions include the compliance with the Building and Town Planning Ordinances; the specification of the gross floor area allowed to be developed; the site coverage percentage (i.e. the percentage of the total site area that can be covered by any building); the maximum number of units, the maximum number of floors; maximum building height above the mean formation level as well as design, disposition and elevation of the development and the deed of mutual covenant and management agreement.

Now, let us look at how some of these conditions are examined from a developer's point of view. From the very beginning stage of the development, one of the most important issues facing the developer and his professional advisers is the calculation of the gross floor area he should build in order to maximize the ceiling control in the lease. We shall use the following example to show how it is analysed.

Assuming a site in urban Kowloon with an area of 5200 sq.ft. which is zoned for residential use with some non-domestic use. There is a building height restriction of 45.72 metres. The permitted domestic plot ratio (PR) is 6 while permitted domestic site coverage is 44%. In addition, the permitted plot ratio for the non-domestic portion is 10.8 with a site coverage allowed at 77.5%.

We can analyse the actual plot ratio as follows:

♦   Height of the site above Hong Kong principal datum (HKPD): 8 m.

♦   Building height therefore: 45.72 m − 8 m. = 37.72 m.

♦   Assuming only two floors of retail use will be developed. As the total floor height does not exceed 15 metres, a maximum site of 100% is allowed by the government for these two retail floors. The retail PR is therefore 2. Hence,

- domestic PR is: $(10.8 - 2) \times 6/10.8 = 4.89$
- total PR is: domestic PR plus retail PR: $4.89 + 2 = 6.89$
- with this PR, the maximum gross floor area allowed to be developed becomes: $6.89 \times$ site area $= 35,828$ sq.ft.
- In addition, we assume the first two retail floors will have a total floor height of 7 metres, and therefore the maximum height for the residential units is: 37.72 m $- 7$ m $= 30.72$ m.
- Furthermore, if the average floor height for the residential floors is about 9 feet, which is approximately 2.73 m, then the maximum number of residential floors is:
- 30.72 m$/2.73$ m $= 11$ storeys
- Hence, in this development, there will be two floors of retail use and 11 floors of residential units. To see if such a proposal violates the maximum limit set in the crown lease, we can work out the maximum floor area as follows:
- GFA for residential: 5200 sq.ft (site area) $\times$ 44% (site coverage) $\times$ 11 storeys $= 25,168$ sq.ft.
- GFA for retail: 5200 sq.ft (site area) $\times$ 100% (site coverage) $\times$ 2 storeys $= 10,400$ sq.ft.
- Total GFA $= 25,168$ sq.ft. $+ 10,400$ sq.ft. $= 35,568$ sq.ft which is below the maximum GFA (35,828 sq.ft. In addition, the actual PR $(2 + 4.84 = 6.84)$ is also below the maximum PR allowed (6.89)

MODIFICATION OF LEASE CONDITIONS IN HONG KONG

We have seen briefly the various types of development controls in the land market and in particular the specific controls set out in the government leases when a developer first buys a piece of land from the government. These controls, however, are not fixed forever. As the environment may change and alter the economic structure of a particular region, some flexibility is needed for the development controls so that the developer may, upon satisfying certain conditions, apply for alteration of the development controls, for instance change of use. This flexibility in the land management system is not only good for the developer but also beneficial to the society as the developer making the application is only responding to the market demand and supply mechanism.

In Hong Kong, modifications of lease controls/conditions are only considered by the Lands Department subject to certain qualifications. One of the prerequisites is that a valid application is being made by one of the following three types of applicants:

1. the registered owner(s);
2. intending purchaser(s) under a registered Agreement for Sale and Purchase and with a written consent given by the registered owner; and
3. the agent of the above two categories with power of attorney.

As mentioned earlier, application for modifications of crown lease conditions may arise out of various circumstances but in most cases, it may come under one of the following items:

*   Modifications arising from conditions imposed by the Town Planning Board:
    Under S.16 of the Town Planning Ordinance (and S.17 of the same Ordinance for appeal), an applicant may apply to the Town Planning Board for a modification of the condition restricting the use of land to that approved by the Board, subject to assessment of premium.
*   Modifications to allow amalgamated development:
    In cases where a merging of two or more lots for joint development purposes necessitates the deletion of non-building areas between two adjacent lots such that all the parking will be on one lot, rather than the appropriate amount on each of the lots, a modification will be considered.
*   Modifications to extinguish government's Right of Way within buildings:
    Crown leases normally reserve rights of ways to the government over common staircases, landings etc. When there is redevelopment of the lot, such common staircases may not be required and hence there is a need for the modification. Government normally allows this provided

that any other lot owners entitled to similar rights make no objection to the extinguishment of rights.

- Modifications arising from relaxation of Airport Height Restriction:
  With the cessation of the density control in 1992 and by virtue of the 1989 Temporary Control of Density of Building Development (Kowloon and New Kowloon) Ordinance, the relaxation of airport height control basically offers no actual benefits to the application except in terms of flexibility of design such as high ceiling etc. Such modifications, however, may be beneficial to commercial and industrial development as it means savings in the construction of basements.
- Modifications for permission of additional number of buildings/floor space:
  This application, upon approval, will normally require assessment of premium.
- Modifications to use non-profit-making school halls for ecclesiastical purposes:
  Upon payment of premium, a modification may be granted for partial or exclusive use of some school (non-profit-making) premises for ecclesiastical purposes, except outside school hours where modification is not necessary as this is granted by the Director of Education.
- Modification to permit the construction of a penthouse.
- Modification to permit removal of non-alienation clause in Civil Servants' Cooperative Building Society Developments.
- Modification to permit the construction of recreational facilities, caretaker's/watchman's offices and/or quarters in residential developments and the residential element of commercial/residential developments.
- Other short term variations of conditions such as restrictive user conditions, etc.

Upon receiving a valid application from one of the three types of applicants, the relevant officials in the Lands Department will check whether there is an unfulfilled building covenant affecting the lot. If this is the case, the Lands Department will normally extend the building covenants for a premium for the period deemed to be adequate to complete the development under the existing lease conditions.

We therefore have seen the mechanism for the application for modifications of lease conditions as well as the common cases where an application will be made. In most of the above circumstances, a premium is required to be paid by the applicant. The basis of the assessment of the premium is the payment of any enhanced land value by the applicant that may arise from the modification. In appraisal terminology, the principle is the "Before and After" valuation model. In assessing the land value (normally based on residual valuation method, see discussion in later chapters), the special factors such as the cost of additional engineering work or other special requirements imposed on the applicant as a result of the modification as well as the saving in development time and construction cost, marriage value[1] and gain in saleable area due to the modification should all be taken into account.

In some cases, however, no premium is required as the modification will not result in enhancement of land value or the modification is solely to the government's advantages.

In some cases, however, modification may result in enhancement of land value which cannot be assessed easily under conventional valuation methods. In such cases, an empirical premium plus normal administrative fee will be charged. The current empirical premium is HK$350,000 with adjustment to a higher or lower figure upon approval of the senior officials such as government land agent in the Lands Department.

One final remark for the assessment of the land premium is that when there is an appeal for re-assessment of land premium from the applicant (which is normally the case), the date of valuation falls on the date of appeal. Hence, it is possible for the assessment of premium to vary substantially from the first offer

---

[1] Marriage value refers to the benefit of additional value to be released from the merging different properties or lots. One of the obvious example is the increase of plot ratio due to the merging of sites.

by the Lands Department when during the negotiation period, the market downward adjusts itself to a great extent. This is in fact what happened in Hong Kong between 1993 and 1995. In one particular case, an application was made at the end of 1993 for a modification of the lease condition user clause from industrial use to industrial/office use in Kwai Chung and an initial offer was made by the Lands Department in 1994. In early 1995, an appeal was made by the applicant's surveyor and the final offer by the Lands Department was 46% lower than the original offer! Hence, the applicant and his agents need to monitor the market closely so as to arrive at the best strategy in negotiating with the relevant authority.

Lease Modification

General rule

A restriction contained in Crown Leases or Conditions of Sale/Conditions of Grants may be waived or modified if there is no contravention of government policy and ordinance. A premium will be payable if the modification enhances the value of the lot.

Application

1. An application for modification will not be considered unless it is made by either:
   a. all the registered owners concerned; or
   b. the intending purchaser under a registered Agreement for Sale and Purchase which is still valid and enforceable at the time of application, subject to the written consent of the registered owner; or
   c. the duly authorized agent of a) or b) above (Letter of Authorization should be obtained).
2. The application is personal to the applicant and any subsequent change in ownership of the lot will automatically invalidate the application.
3. Application for a major modification of a lease sold at full market value by auction or tender will not normally be considered within a certain period from the date of

sale, unless the application is supported by justifications accepted by the Government Land Agent (GLA).

4. A re-application made within one year of the date of withdrawal of the original application will not be considered (subject to market conditions).

Consideration

The modification will only be processed subject to the following:

1. No contravention of Laws and Ordinances.
2. Consistent with current Town Plan.
3. No contravention of government policy (e.g. Density Zones, Special Control Areas and Moratorium Areas etc.).
4. The restriction of out-dated or spent of effect.

Usual Procedures in the Government Department (Lands Department)

1. To seek the approval of the relevant Policy Branch, if necessary (where concessionary grant or deviation of normal policy are involved).
2. To circulate the proposed modification, incorporating up-to-date development conditions not already included in the current Leases or Conditions of Sale etc., to the interested Departments for comment.
3. To submit the basic terms together with any development conditions imposed by other Departments to the District Lands Committee (DLC) for consideration.
4. To issue a letter incorporating the proposed basic terms and draft special conditions for the applicants' information and acceptance.
5. To assess the modification premium and administrative fee following DLC approval.
6. To issue a formal offer letter incorporating the agreed basic terms and premium with a demand note for the administrative fee within one month of approval of the premium assessment.
7. The offer is to be made in the following way:

    a.   Basic terms are open for acceptance for 1 month only. (District Lands Officer DLO may approve a longer period for a major and complicated modification).

    b.   The administrative fee is to be paid within 1 month.

    c.   The transaction is to be completed within 6 months

8.   Upon acceptance of the basic terms and payment of the administrative fee, the modification documents will be finalized by the specified date. The District Land Surveyor should be requested to prepare plans for attachment to the documents if necessary.

9.   Issue a demand note for the premium and modification documents to the owner for execution allowing payment within 21 days if the premium is not more than 1 million and within 28 days if the premium is in excess of 1 million.

10. Execute the modification document on behalf of government and return a copy to the DLO for the records after registration.

Premium Assessment

The basic principle is that the owner is required to pay for any enhancement in the land value of his lot which arises as a result of the modification. The method of valuation will normally be a direct comparison of the "Before value" and "After value" of the land.

Date of assessment of premium

Assessment is normally on the basis of current date value.

1.   *Nil Assessment of Premium*

    Assessment is nil when the modification will not result in any enhancement of land value (a technical modification) or when the modification is solely to the government's advantage (Provision of open space or government facilities in the development as required under S.16 of Town Planning Ordinance)

    The following are examples of technical modifications:

a. Modification from "industrial" to "industrial/godown" purposes.
b. Removal of prohibition on alienation for lots sold at public auction.
c. Provision of canteens in industrial buildings (not exceeding 10% of the total gross floor area GFA of the building).
d. Extinguishment of the right of way reserved for the government over common staircases and landings in existing buildings (subject to the agreement of adjoining owners who are entitled to similar rights).
e. Removal of an Offensive Trade Clause and Rate of Range Clause.
f. Construction of swimming pool in land restricted to garden use.
g. Where the modification is for charity purposes.

2. *Empirical Premium Modification*
Where the modification will result in enhancement which cannot be assessed by normal valuation methods, the empirical premium plus normal administrative fee will be charged. The current empirical premium is fixed at HK$350,000 but GLA or Principal GLA has discretion to decide a higher or lower figure for a particular case as he sees fit. Examples of empirical premium cases:
a. Provision of a swimming pool on a non-building area.
b. Reduction of parking spaces to the current standard.
c. Deletion of non-building areas between two lots to allow provision of all parking spaces within one lot rather than the appropriate amount on each of the lots.
d. Diversion/improvement of an existing pedestrian right of way where it will not result in increase of development potential.

3. *Full Premium Modification*
Where the increase in land value can be identified by direct comparison of "After value" with "Before value,"

the full amount of increase should be charged. The value of land required to be surrendered and the cost of any additional engineering work or other special require-ments imposed on the lot owner as a result of the modification should be taken into account, as well as time and construction cost, marriage value and gain in saleable area due to the modification.

4.   *Buy-Back Basis*
Where the modification is to regulate an existing breach of lease condition, a panel buy back approach is to be adopted in premium calculation. Examples of such cases are regularization of unauthorized penthouse and addi-tional storeys resulting in excessive GFA. This principle only applies to structures having an independent saleable value. For structures incapable of being separately sold, the premium should be based on the enhanced land value with interest payable from the date of the breach.

Premium review and appeal

1.   The premium should be offered within 1 month from the date of approval of the premium assessment.
2.   The premium should be reviewed if the transaction is not completed within 6 months from the date of offer, whether the delay be on the part of the applicant or of the government.
3.   Upon appeal, the premium will be re-assessed at the date of the appeal.
4.   The appeal should be considered by an officer of con-ference of higher level than the ones who approved the original premium.
5.   If the appeal is considered to be unsupported by facts and other justification, it should be rejected and the 6-month premium review period will be unaffected.

If the appeal is supported by facts or justification, the 6 months premium review period will be suspended during the period of appeal.

The following figures explain the various procedures in

Figure 11 Flow Chart for Processing a Development Project

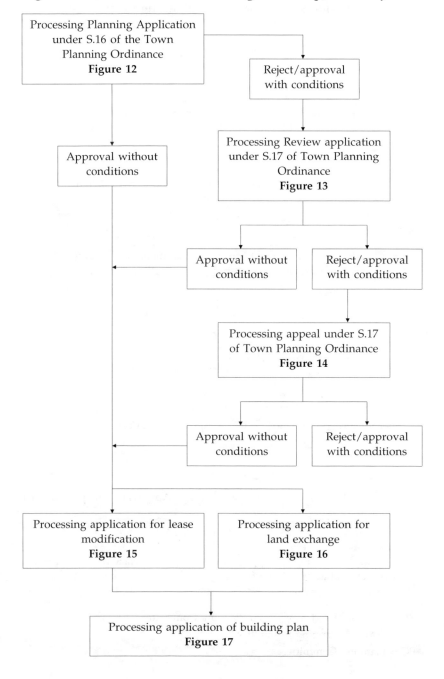

Figure 12 Procedures for Processing a Planning Application under S.16 of the Town Planning Ordinance

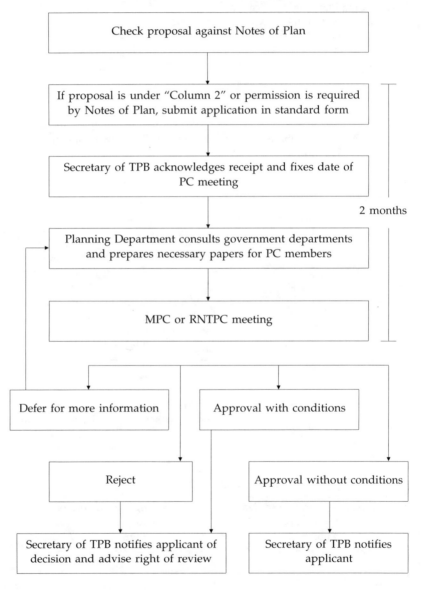

RNTPC = Rural and New Town Planning Committee
MPC = Metro Planning Committee
PC = Planning Committee

Figure 13 Procedures for Processing a Review Application under S.17 of the Town Planning Ordinance

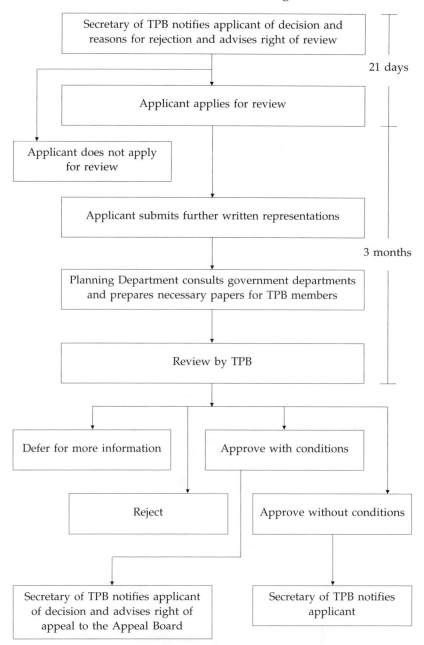

Figure 14 Procedures for Processing and Appeal under S.17 of the Town Planning Ordinance

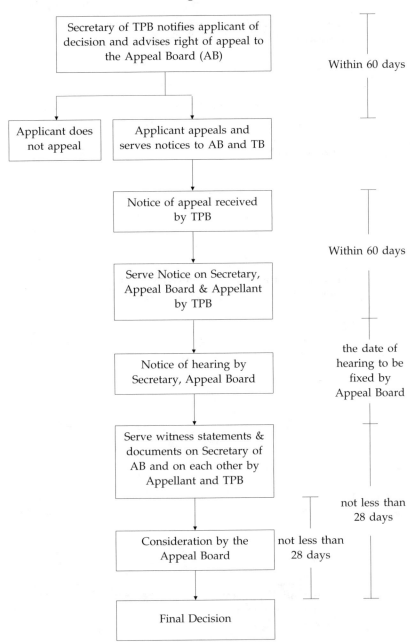

Figure 15 Procedures for Processing a Lease Modification

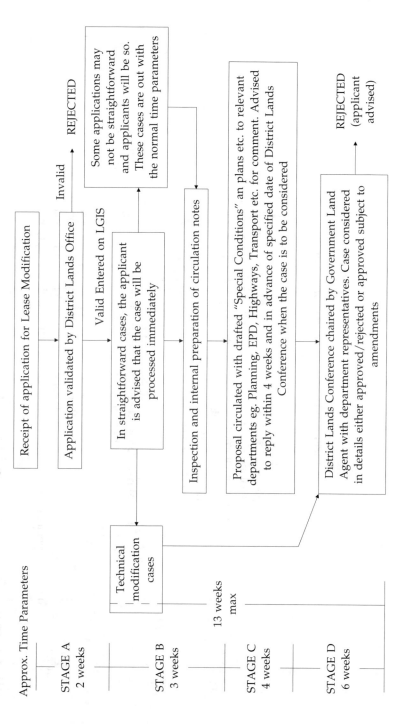

Approx. Time Parameters

Receipt of application for Lease Modification

Application validated by District Lands Office

Invalid → REJECTED

Valid Entered on LGIS

In straightforward cases, the applicant is advised that the case will be processed immediately

Some applications may not be straightforward and applicants will be so. These cases are out with the normal time parameters

Technical modification cases

Inspection and internal preparation of circulation notes

Proposal circulated with drafted "Special Conditions" an plans etc. to relevant departments eg. Planning, EPD, Highways, Transport etc. for comment. Advised to reply within 4 weeks and in advance of specified date of District Lands Conference when the case is to be considered

District Lands Conference chaired by Government Land Agent with department representatives. Case considered in details either approved/rejected or approved subject to amendments

REJECTED (applicant advised)

STAGE A
2 weeks

STAGE B
3 weeks

13 weeks max

STAGE C
4 weeks

STAGE D
6 weeks

Figure 15 (Cont'd)

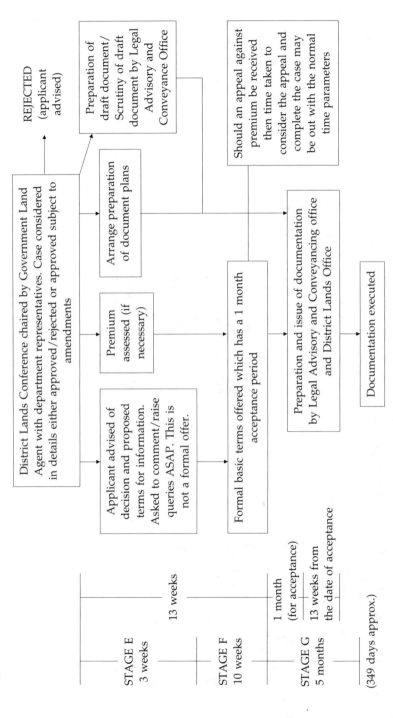

Figure 16 Procedures for Processing a Land Exchange

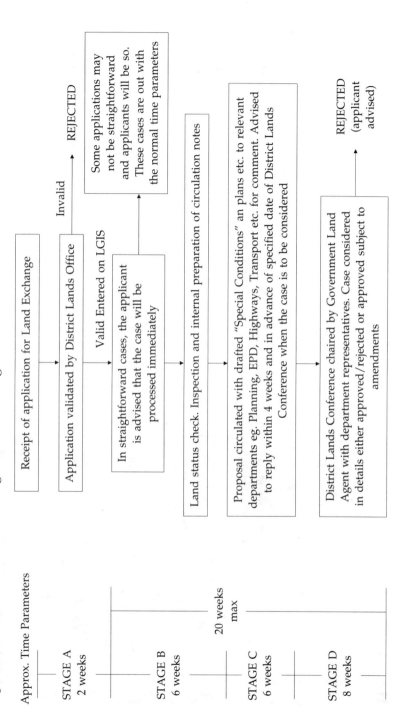

Figure 16 (Cont'd)

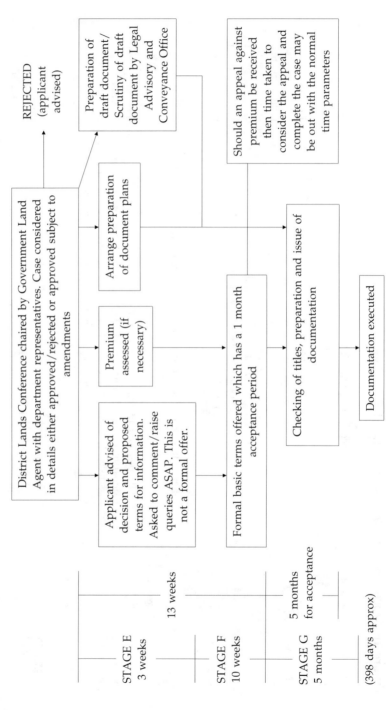

STAGE E
3 weeks

13 weeks

STAGE F
10 weeks

5 months
for acceptance

STAGE G
5 months

(398 days approx)

Figure 17 Procedures for Processing Building Plans

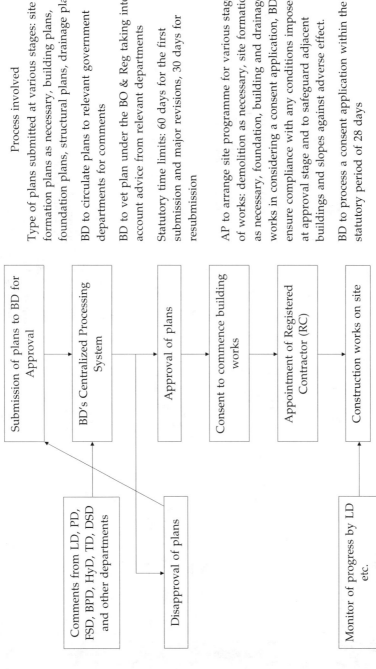

Process involved	
Submission of plans to BD for Approval	Type of plans submitted at various stages: site formation plans as necessary, building plans, foundation plans, structural plans, drainage plans
BD's Centralized Processing System	BD to circulate plans to relevant government departments for comments
	BD to vet plan under the BO & Reg taking into account advice from relevant departments
	Statutory time limits: 60 days for the first submission and major revisions, 30 days for resubmission
Approval of plans	
Consent to commence building works	AP to arrange site programme for various stages of works: demolition as necessary, site formation as necessary, foundation, building and drainage works in considering a consent application, BD to ensure compliance with any conditions imposed at approval stage and to safeguard adjacent buildings and slopes against adverse effect.
Appointment of Registered Contractor (RC)	BD to process a consent application within the statutory period of 28 days
Construction works on site	

Comments from LD, PD, FSD, BPD, HyD, TD, DSD and other departments

Disapproval of plans

Monitor of progress by LD etc.

Figure 17 (Cont'd)

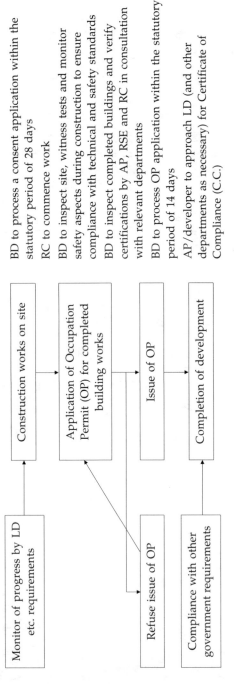

Monitor of progress by LD etc. requirements

Construction works on site

BD to process a consent application within the statutory period of 28 days

RC to commence work

Application of Occupation Permit (OP) for completed building works

BD to inspect site, witness tests and monitor safety aspects during construction to ensure compliance with technical and safety standards

BD to inspect completed buildings and verify certifications by AP, RSE and RC in consultation with relevant departments

Refuse issue of OP

Issue of OP

BD to process OP application within the statutory period of 14 days

Compliance with other government requirements

Completion of development

AP/developer to approach LD (and other departments as necessary) for Certificate of Compliance (C.C.)

LD: Lands Department
PD: Planning Department
BD: Buildings Department
FSD: Fire Services Department
EPD: Environmental Protection Dept.
HyD: Highways Department
TD: Transport Department
DSD: Drainage Services Department
BO: Building Ordinances
OP: Occupation Permit

making these applications. However, it should be emphasized here that there is a review process going on in the planning procedure and once the review is approved officially, some of these flow charts may not be applicable as they will be stream-lined in the future.

CASE STUDY

A standard approach (Before and After Valuation) adopted by the government in assessment land premium will be similar to the following:

Before Application Value

GDV (existing use):
 s.f. @$
 P.V. _____ years @ _____%   _____

Less development costs:

1. Construction costs s.f. @$
2. Professional fees   @6% of item (1)
3. Developer's profit   @20% of (1) and (2)
    P.V. _____ years @ _____%

          Land and Profit _____

Divided by 20% profit rate   divided by 1.2

      = Before Land value _____

After Application Value

GDV (new use):
 s.f. @$
 P.V. _____ years @ _____%   _____

Less development costs

1. Construction costs s.f. @$
2. Professional fees   @6% of item (1)

3. Developer's profit   @20% of (1) and (2)
        P.V. _____ years @ _____%

                                        Land and Profit _____
Divided by 20% profit rate   divided by 1.2

                              = After Land value _____

Land Premium = Before Land Value minus After Land Value
where:

1. GDV is the gross development value representing the total value of the completed development which is either the gross proceeds of the sale of the completed properties or the gross capitalized rental values of the properties if they are not for sale (see later chapters on property appraisal).

2. P.V. is the professional jargon for Present Value. It is the discounting process for converting all future incomes into today's values.

This simple residual model of valuation assumes that the gross development value, although based on current market price of similar properties, is receivable only after the completion of the development. Hence, we need to discount this value to the present date's basis. The same is assumed for construction costs and professional fees. This is necessary as we need to find the present date land value. The final item of deduction (i.e. the profit rate of 20%) is the developer's profit on the land. In the process of this valuation, the government standardizes the developer's profit at 20%.

When surveyors are dealing with the government, it is necessary to follow the government approach. Hence, in this case study, the surveyor, in trying to estimate the premium payable to the government due to the modification of the lease conditions will carry out the following calculation:

This is a simple case of lease modification where the owner of the existing building is applying for a relaxation of the height restriction from the Lands Department. In addition, he also applies for permission to reserve space for car-parking facilities.

No. 128 Industry Road, Kwun Tong, Kowloon
Premium Calculation for Lease Modification

Valuation Date	:	31st March 1995
Property	:	No. 128 Industry Road, Kwun Tong Kowloon
Lot Area	:	1005.2 sq m (10,820 sq ft)
Net Site Area	:	1005.2 sq m (10,820 sq ft)
Class of the Site	:	Class A
Airport Height Limit	:	130 m above PD
Spot Level	:	Approx 4.2 m above PD
Permitted Bldg Height	:	Approx 51.8 m above PD
Town Planning Use	:	Industrial (S/K 14S/5)
Proposed Scheme	:	14 Storey Industrial Building
Non Building Area	:	820 sq ft at the rear

Before Modification

Residual Valuation Method

Gross Development Value (GDV)

	SFA	$/SFA (saleable floor area)	
G/F	5,973	$4,500	$ 26,878,500
1/F	9,457	$2,400	$ 22,696,800
2/F–3/F	18,913	$2,250	$ 42,554,250
4/F–13/F	66,007	$2,110	$139,274,770
	GDV on Completion		$231,404,320
PV 2 yrs @ 11%		0.8116	$187,807,746

Construction Cost

	GFA		
Ind. Bldg	119,020	600	$ 71,412,000
Professional Fee		6%	$ 4,284,720
Profit & Risk		20%	$ 15,139,344
	$90,836,064		
PV 1 yr @ 11%		0.9009	$ 81,834,210
Residual Value			$105,973,536
Deduct Profit		20%	1.2
		$88,311,280	
	Say	$88,310,000	

After Modification

Residual Valuation Method
Gross Development Value

	SFA/No.	$/SFA (saleable floor area)	
Lorry cps	7	$ 600,000	$ 4,200,000
Private cps	7	$1,000,000	$ 7,000,000
G/F	4,869	$ 4,800	$ 23,371,200
3/F–22/F	98,678	$ 2,190	$216,104,820
	GDV on Completion		$250,676,020
PV 2 yrs @ 11%		0.8116	$203,676,020

Construction Cost

	GFA		
CPS	28,370	350	$ 9,929,500
Ind. Bldg	129,840	630	$81,799,200
Professional Fee		6%	$ 5,503,722
Profit & Risk		20%	$19,446,484
	$106,749,406		
PV 1 yr @ 11%		0.9009	$ 96,170,540
Residual Value			$107,278,118
Allow Profit		20%	1.2
			$89,398,431
	Say		$89,400,000

Therefore: Premium payable

	GFA	
After Value	119,020 sq ft	$89,400,000
Before Value	129,840 sq ft	$88,310,000
Premium Payable to Government		$ 1,090,000

The logic of this "before and after" approach is to find the difference between the value of land after modification of the lease conditions. In principle, no developer will go through the application procedure unless there is a potential gain after the lease modification process. Since the site was bought on the basis of the existing use and lease conditions, the developer will need to compensate the government for the change of the original lease conditions.

Chapter 3

Appraisal of Real Estate: A Theoretical Framework

"Appraisal" or "valuation" is conventionally translated into Chinese as *gujia* which literally means "price guessing." This term is generally adopted in Hong Kong, Taiwan and mainland China. This does not help very much in defining the exact rationale of appraisal. All chartered surveyors know that there is the investment method of appraisal, cost approach, as well as residual valuation. But these are only techniques and models. What exactly is property appraisal? Rarely do we find a full discussion of why appraisal is needed. Before going into the details of the appraisal process, one should therefore give some attention to the rationale of appraisal.

Appraisal can be described as a process of estimating marketing value, investment value, insurable value or other properly defined values of an identified interest or interests in a specific parcel or parcels of real estate at a given date (Akerson, 1984, p. 148).

This seems to be quite vague. Baum and Mackmin (1989) give a better interpretation of the "process":

> ... Valuation is a process which requires careful consideration of a number of variables before figures can be substituted in mathematically proven formula.... Any assessment of present worth or market value can only be as good as the data input allows and that factor is dependent upon the education, skill and experience of the valuer. Ability to analyze and understand the market is of paramount importance....

This process is best described as appraisal or evaluation. This may make the situation clearer. By appraisal is meant a process of information collection; selection; organization, analysis and eventually conclusion. Analysis is an essential and vital part in this process before getting to this conclusion. Some, however, may regard this process as pure market comparison, and there need not be any analysis. Fraser (1988) argues that:

> ... it is irrelevant to market valuation whether the market is ignorant or irrational. In a relatively inefficient market like the property market, a valuer's opinion of a property's value may well be more sensible and rational than the market's but he can't arrive at a better market value than does the market itself ... the process of market valuation is essentially a process of comparison. In the majority of cases it is neither necessary nor desirable to undertake an analysis of variables which determine value....

The divergence in the approaches in the treatment of the appraisal process comes from the fact that appraisal is always broken down into different exercises or aspects depending on the objectives. Fraser (1988) demonstrates this point by saying:

> ... if the objective is to carry out an appraisal for investment decision-making, the valuation will be the valuer's own view of the property's worth, and should reflect his views on such variables as rental growth, obsolescence, and risk. But if the objective is market valuation, then the personal views of the valuer on such matters are irrelevant. The valuation exercise is essentially one of the objective comparison and only those variables which have been quantified from comparable sales evidence should be incorporated....

This makes appraisal only a practical way to solve problems within an established market system. But this will not make appraisal a theoretical way to analyse problems. There is therefore a need to elaborate "appraisal" *per se*.

Whenever there is a need to find value, it is a matter of appraisal. Appraisal, therefore, should aim at getting the value, not price. This is exactly what the term "valuation" implies. There is no estimation of price, although there is an estimation of possible price. This is because price can only be realized through actual market transaction.

OBJECTIVES OF APPRAISAL

Appraisal evolves from capitalistic economic theories, it has its own set of assumptions, notably the open market value assumptions. Notwithstanding the fact that not all of these assumptions can be realized even in the capitalist market, they are important.

Appraisal is a discipline of philosophy. Like Economics and Management, it has different branches of theories and applications. Attention is usually diverted to an individual purpose/aspect of appraisal. Hence each of these methods can only explain part of the market to the extent that the assumptions behind them can go. To examine the role and application of appraisal techniques under a different economic system, the rationale *per se* should be understood.

Appraisal literally means the finding of the value, not price. There is a basic difference as well as relationship between them. The market is the place where value is transformed into a common indicator of trend — price — through a series of negotiations and legal proceedings.

Value invariably involves the use-value of the property. Price is concerned mainly with the opportunity cost of acquisition due to scarcity of resources. In the property market, it is easy to have a situation where opportunity cost exceeds use value substantially. In such a situation, value cannot elaborate the market situation when market appraisal is only concerned with transaction price.

Value should be taken as an element to help the decision making and analysis process, while price is the decision made after this process. To use Marx's words, the measure of value exists before exchange.

Appraisal is not about the mathematical process through which a statistically precise figure can be created and proved. It is about the explanation of the interrelationship between the different variables in the real estate market from the micro level and in the economy from the macro level. Without such an understanding, the application of appraisal is very restrictive. Brown (1991) remarks that:

> ... the correct role of valuation models is to define the economic relationship between the relevant variables in order to arrive at values which could establish a market in equilibrium.... The principle function of valuation models in this context therefore is to establish whether

individual properties offered for sale are either under- or over-priced relative to their equilibrium market values ... valuation is drafted in terms of expectations and is a reflection on the quality and the amount of information....

APPRAISAL MODELS: AN INTRODUCTION

Techniques in appraisal should only be viewed as devices to elaborate different aspects of "value" under different assumptions. In general, these various methods will obtain the open market value. But due to their different emphasis, the value obtained is different. Hence, the degree of representation varies.

Market Comparison Method

Baum and Mackmin (1989) regard appraisal by direct capital comparison with sales in the market as the preferred method of appraisal, provided that the sample of comparable sales is of a sufficient size to draw realistic conclusions as to market conditions.

This can only happen, as mentioned in the previous section, when the market is truly competitive. When this is the case, market price itself reflects truly the worth of the property. The theory behinds this is that market is the central place where buyers and sellers, after ascertaining in their mind the value/worth of the property, negotiate with each other. And eventually, all the "value" will be translated into a common form of measurement: market price. This market price would measure the mental state of the market as at the date of appraisal.

On the other hand, when the input data does not make any sense, the output result i.e. the "value" shows only the fact that some people in the market are willing to pay for a certain sum of money for a particular purpose.

This disintegrates appraisal into pieces of techniques each capable of explaining only one part of the market, but cannot figure the interrelationship of the different elements in the market. A classic example is the residential market in Hong Kong. Prices have been rocketing since the end of 1990 representing a substantial rise in asset demand while rental movement has remained sluggish throughout the whole period. A substantial gap is created between the asset market and the rental market. This can only be justified by the fact that some sector of the population is willing to pay for that much and is giving the value as such. But it fails to explain why this is the case.

The biggest advantage of market comparison approach is that it is easy and quick. In fact, in most other kinds of appraisal techniques, there is always an element of comparison. There is a need to find rental income and market yield by comparison in the investment approach as well as in residual valuation. There is also a need to find cost data in the contractor's approach. To a certain extent, therefore, comparison is the main core in appraisal. It is the preferred way to obtain data, as the first step of the appraisal process. This method is best for finding the possible price of small standardized units like residential units of the same block.

In some cases, some might argue, market price is more important than analysis of the property worth, such as in the case of mortgage valuation for ordinary residential property. In such cases, market price is the only value one should look for. This however, is not the case. When a purchaser invests a sum of money in a residential property, he/she is doing this for one or more of the following three purposes:

1.   owner-occupation;
2.   long term investment,
3.   quick capital gains.

The first two objectives require the surveyor to find the "worth" of the property to this investor in the form of either opportunity cost of occupation or alternative investment opportunities.

It is true that in both of these cases, the purchaser has to know the market price, but it also matters that this purchaser knows the assumptions and implications of such a value obtained by this appraisal process. As Darlow (1983) comments that:

> ... the valuer is often not quantifying or questioning his assumptions ... it matters a great deal to an investor who is attempting to calculate whether property in general, or a specific property, is likely to show

him a better "Internal Rate of Return" than the alternative investments available. It matters also when an investor is trying to calculate what price he could afford to pay for a property to show him a certain required IRR....

This is because the real estate market is never in a static state. Market price keeps changing with the changes in the assumptions and expectations of the market. Unless the purchaser is looking for, and in fact can achieve, a quick sale, the value obtained by comparison cannot exemplify the implications of the market changes.

This does not only apply to investors (long term), it also describes the case for owner-occupation. When a person is purchasing a house for actual occupation, the price he is going to pay should reflect his long term saving and spending plan. When the housing is substantially over-priced, this affects the long term loan repayments. In this situation, the opportunity of purchasing the house outweighs the rental payment if he rents a house instead.

There is, hence, a potential conflict in the appraisal practice. When such a purchaser goes to the bank and tries to get a mortgage loan, the bank's mortgage valuation section will carry out a normal mortgage valuation which is based mainly on market price comparison. Few banks will actually ask the purchaser whether he is looking for a quick capital gain, occupation or long term investment. A value obtained in this way, will cause a potential loss with regard to the two latter objectives, i.e. the purchaser may have to pay more than is received every month.

The Income Approach or Investment Appraisal

The notion that capital value is expressed as a function of future rental income is well recognized both by the Marxist economists:

> ... rent exists whether land is the object of exchange or not. If there is exchange, the price of the land is determined by the rent discounted at the current interest rate.... (Abraham-Frois and Berribi, 1979, p. 94)

and by the property professionals:

... The basic principles of property value suggest the existence of a predictable relationship between income and value. Knowing that real estate is only one of many investment opportunities, the behaviour of buyers and sellers in other investment markets should give us a clue about the income/value relationship.... If a plausible relationship between income and value can be estimated when only the income is known.... (Akerson, 1984, pp. 6–7)

This provides a certain logic in arriving at the value of the property. At least it gives a guarantee that the income to be generated from the property will be able to compensate for the cost of owning the property. This gives a clearer picture of the relationship of the different elements in the appraisal process. This logic has long been recognized by the well-established economic theory of capital value, as when Fisher (1930) gives his idea of what capital value is:

... 1) capital value is income capitalized or discounted, 2) if the rate of interest falls, the capital value rises and vise versa, 3) This rise or fall in capital value is relatively great for durable goods like land, ... 4) capital value is increased by savings, the income being decreased by the same amount that the capital is increased. 5) These savings thus diverted from income and turned back into capital will, except for mischance, be the basis for real income later....

In the simplest form, the income approach means the summation of all future rental income. The process of summation is called capitalization which takes the present value of the future income into consideration. In fact, the income approach is the closest of property appraisal techniques to the investment and financial world. In the stock market, for example, the price/earning ratio (PER) has long been a common measurement for investment decisions. PER is actually the same as Year Purchase in the British system of the appraisal profession. The income approach is also the area in appraisal theory which attracts most academic research (Wood, 1972; Crosby, 1985).

Basically, there are three major elements in this model, namely, the rental income; the capitalization yield and the holding period. The latter two will work out a multiplier — Years' Purchase in the UK appraisal terminology, or Income Multiplier in the US system — which the annual income is then multiplied by to produce the capital value. In Fisher's terms, this means:

> ... the price of income in terms of capital ... is called the "rate of years" namely the number of years during which there would flow an amount of income equal to the capital....

Both the yield and the rental income can be found from market data. The holding period is specific to the subject property. In this way, when these three elements work together, there is market analysis as well as factors concerned specifically with the subject property.

In addition, these three elements each have their own assumptions. Capitalization yield is only a general analysis of the market relationship between rental and capital value. It is time specific, for the all-risk yield represents the ratio between the open market rack rent and the open market value at a particular point of time. As time goes by, they are bound to become outdated as data.

As this yield decides the magnitude of the Income Multiplier factor to a certain extent, the adjustment of yield (when valuing a particular property) becomes very important. This adjustment depends on a set of assumptions each of which contribute to the final "shape" of the figure. These include the growth factor during the term and reversion, the rent review pattern, and the risk element. Among all these, the growth factor is especially important for this is the element which defines the meaning of implied all risk yield for capitalization. This is also the area which distinguishes between equated yield (or rate of return) and all risk yield.

This also distinguishes the difference between such traditional UK appraisal models as the term and reversion method and the development of modern financial appraisal methods. The underlying debate is actually whether appraisal should be taken as market comparison or as investment appraisal. This will be discussed later in detail.

Residual Valuation

Appraisal of land value is the theme of this book and will be discussed in detail in later chapters. Land value as discussed earlier is regarded as a residual value. This originates from a concept in land economics. This is that land is a fixed element, payment for which would be made when a residual value is obtained after all the costs and liabilities are deducted from the total revenue. Land value therefore depends very much on the nature of the economic activities undertaken on the land and production costs.

The model seems so logical and justified. But in the UK, the Lands Tribunal has denounced this method as far from a certain guide to values (Baum and Mackmin, 1989, p. 181). This is mainly due to the fact that there are so many variables in the model, and they are interrelated. Hence, a change in any one or some of these variables will invariably exert a greater effect on the final residual value. Because of this risk, there is a high possibility of fluctuation in the land value.

On the other hand, if we look at this problem from another angle it is not that pessimistic. It is just because there are so many elements in the model that the analyst needs a very careful approach to identify the assumptions behind each element. Of course, land value can be obtained by strict comparison of market land prices from previous transactions. This, however, is not the rationale of the model. The rationale behind the residual valuation model is to assess the residual process. There must be an ideal "economic activity" to be carried out on the land. There is no way to compare the price of two pieces of land without any reference to the different elements in the residual model unless these two pieces of land are absolutely identical in size, use, design layout and development and management.

When we are applying the residual valuation method, it should be the rationale of the model we are looking for instead of the mechanical process of calculation. In this model, land is regarded as a fixed element in the development process. As with to the Ricardian theory of land rent,[1] the value of land is a residual element, i.e. the value is whatever is left after allowances are

---

[1] For a detailed discussion of the theory of land value, see Evans (1988a).

made for all other charges and liabilities. Any appraisal based on this model should bear this in mind.

Profit Method

This model is similar to the residual valuation method in some ways, but deviates in some other areas. Both this method and the residual valuation method emphasize the importance of the economic activities on the land. Residual valuation is about the land itself while the profit method is about the property on the land.

The assumptions behind this model are that people purchase or rent a property for the sole purpose of carrying out business activities which will generate income. Income thus comes from the economic activities, not from the properties built on land. Land is a factor of production contributing to the profitability of business, as payment for land is directly linked to the amount of net profit. It is assumed that a portion of the net profit will go to the owner of property which contributes to the profit by way of locational advantages.

Hence, the biggest consideration in valuing these properties is the nature of the business activities carried out on the property. This is affected by the way in which these businesses earn income, e.g. by the number of people entering a property such as a cinema, or by the money people spend inside a property such as a hotel.

The aim of this process is to find the portion of the net profit going into the rent. This rental figure will then be capitalized to find the capital value. So in theory, the valuation process is actually similar to that of the investment method.

Cost Approach

Value is not equal to cost, this is the basic appraisal principle. This approach is used when property value is based on the cost of production, or when the value of the property is regarded as a strict factor of production. It therefore does not take into consideration how much the property can be sold for.

To achieve such a cost, an estimation of the land value is

done based on the vacant site. The appraisal of the superstructure is based on the reinstatement cost or the replacement cost of the existing property, allowing for the obsolescence and depreciation factors. The reason for valuing the property in this way is to illustrate the use value to the owner at its existing state of physical, economical and functional adaptability. The biggest problem therefore is to value the cost of building a new structure exactly the same as the existing one. There is a need to adjust the degree of obsolescence and depreciation in different areas. In fact, there is much controversy about the assessment of obsolescence as it relates to new replacement cost (Albritton, 1982, p. 77).

We have briefly discussed the various common appraisal models from above. It is, however, not the intention of the author to distinguish the effectiveness of any particular model. Different models are particularly suitable for certain circumstances. For instance, where there is no market data at all and where the subject property is not usually traded in the market, the application of the cost approach will at least give an indication of the cost needed to rebuild a similar structure. However, these circumstances are not very common (except for example when the management board of a church decides to turn the church into a limited company for taxation purposes. There will then be a need to value the physical structure of the church as an asset. In this situation, the church will be valued on the basis of cost). Under most circumstances, property ownership involves a certain degree of investment consideration (even if initially there was a sole need for shelter). Hence, to look at the value of real estate from an investment point of view becomes a natural tendency for a proper measurement of real estate value. As we understand that land value is of a residual nature, which depends on the value of properties on land, there will be a need to discuss the assessment of property values based on investment appraisal before examining the appraisal of land value. In the next chapter, we will be looking at the investment appraisal model in detail.

APPRAISAL OF REAL ESTATE VALUE

In carrying out development appraisal of land, one must first understand how much the completed development can generate in terms of income. This is in fact the gross sale value of the properties built on the site. For most kinds of properties, there are basically two common methods of finding the values of real estate. The first is by comparison and the second one is by investment appraisal. The comparison method is relatively easy and simple as explained earlier. So long as we have an active market with abundant recent market transaction data of the similar properties, this method is reliable. However, there are some other cases where the rental market is more active than the capital market, such as the grade A office market. In this case, we could try the investment appraisal method to estimate the open market value of the property.

The Investment Appraisal Model

The basic logic in investment appraisal is the understanding that money has a time value. Money receivable in the future is worth less than the same amount of money receivable today. Hence, the present value (PV) of one dollar receivable after n years at an interest rate (or discount rate) of i is worth:

$$PV = \frac{1}{(1+i)^n} \qquad [1]$$

The product of formula [1] can be called a PV factor. Any future value of a sum of money can be multiplied by this factor to find the present value. The PV factor is always less than 1 because future value is always less than present value. The reasons for this are mainly twofold. One is the opportunity cost in expected future value. Opportunity cost is the return forgone on other investment opportunities when investing in a particular project. For instance, say Mr Bean has HK$100 and he invests all this sum into project A. The opportunity cost for this decision is the likely return he can have from projects B, C or D. So long as project A compensates him enough, or the opportunity cost is less than the return from project A, Mr Bean should be a happy man. In the present value situation, the utility of immediate consumption is always greater than deferred consumption. Hence future value is less than present value.

The second reason is even more straightforward. In the age of inflation, future value is always readily eroded by inflation in terms of purchasing power. As a result, money receivable now is worth more than the same amount in the future.

In fact, the PV factor formula can be analysed in reverse. For instance, say we have HK$100 today and invest this sum into a regular investment giving a 10% return per annum. In one year's time, we will have HK$110 (since HK$100 × [1 + 10%] = HK$110). In this case, 10% is our required rate of return. Now, let us look at this from the future. If we are given an opportunity to receive HK$110 in one year's time, how much are we prepared to pay for such opportunity? Since we can earn 10% from a regular investment, we will use 10% as the discount rate to find the present value. As a result, the present value of HK$110 in a year's time is: HK$110 × 1/(1 + 10%) = HK$100.

In the simplest form, the investment value of a property will equate to the worth of the future earnings. The theory is that no investor will pay for more than he can earn from the investment. As a result, the earning capacity (i.e. rental income) of the property is the main independent variable in the valuation model. This also fits into conventional economic wisdom as Ratcliff (1949) puts it:

> ... sale price, the price that a buyer normally is willing to pay after considering alternatives, represents the present or discount value of future values. The cost of ownership is a function of both contract rent and sales price, the owner must recognize a cost of occupancy that is at least as great as the rental income might otherwise be receiving if he were to rent out his property and no smaller than the total interest on the investment, taxes, maintenance and depreciation, which total, in the long run, is in balance with rental value. The market price of space, over the long run is basically an expression of its productivity or to be more realistic, of the forecasts of men with respect to its future productivity....

The following formula provides for the basic valuation model for a property which produces income at the end of the first year and is to be sold at that moment:

$$V = \frac{I}{(1 + i)} + \frac{P}{(1 + i)} \qquad [2]$$

Where V is the investment value, I is the income obtained at the end of year one; P is the resale's price and i is discount rate. A major controlling variable from this formula is the discount rate. It is a controlling variable in the sense that it decides the magnitude of discount of the future values. It also provides for the measurement standard which helps in the comparison of capital value on the same basis of present value.

According to Fisher (1930), interest rates are made up of three components namely time preference; risk and inflation. A simple way to get this interest rate is to add a premium onto the best lending rate. This represents the cost of capital. The reason for choosing this rate is to guarantee that the rental income can cover the cost of borrowing. This is especially important when most investments are heavily leveraged. The use of the cost of the capital interest rate to discount the future value will give the investor a guarantee that the cost of occupancy is self-financed during the holding period.

This means that the value of a property is equal to the sum of the present values of its income receivable at the end of the holding period and that of the resale price. On the other hand, if the income flow continues for a certain period before resale, the formula becomes:

$$V = \frac{I1}{(1+i)} + \frac{I2}{(1+i)^2} + \dots \frac{In+P}{(1+i)^n} \qquad [3]$$

Where I1, I2 and In are the rental values in the first, second and nth year respectively. P is the reversionary sale price.

Brown (1991) uses a slightly complicated approach in interpreting the above formula by using the expected rate of return to discount the second year income and so on. This in theory would reflect the investor's perception of future time preferences, risks and inflation expectations. However, it is obvious that as the holding period gets longer, the number of discount rates used increases such that by the time it gets to year n, the income and the reversionary value will have to be discounted by a whole series of rates, which is not very practical.

When the income is fixed within the holding period, the capital value of the interest during the holding period then becomes:

$$V = \frac{1 - PV}{i} * I \qquad\qquad\qquad [4]$$

It is also obvious that when the holding approaches infinity, the reversionary capital value approaches zero, hence it becomes relatively insignificant. Where PV is the present value factor $(PV = \frac{1}{(1 + i)^n})$ for the holding period, i is the discount rate and I is the annual income.

In infinity, PV of the reversionary capital value approaches 0 such that formula [3] becomes:

$$V = \frac{I}{i} \qquad\qquad\qquad [5]$$

In both formulae [4] and [5], the first portion on the right hand side of the equation (i.e $\frac{1 - PV}{i}$ in [4] and $\frac{1}{i}$ in [5]) is known as Years' Purchase or YP in the British surveying profession. In the US appraiser's profession, it is known as the Gross Income Multiplier. It represents the present value of a series of 1 dollar payments receivable at the end of each year for n years in [4] or until eternity in [5]. The annual income is multiplied by this factor to arrive at a capital value for the property and hence the real estate value.

This elaborates fully the fact that capital value is a function of the rental income and the interest rate, i.e. the higher the income, the lower the interest rate (hence discount rate) and the higher the capital value (hence the higher the price an investor can offer) for the property. More importantly, it elaborates the fact that capital value can be ascertained by the initial income I.

The above formulae establish the capital value when either the rental income is fixed for the holding period or the income is fixed until infinity. Where rental income is fixed only between rent reviews but inflates at growth rate after reviews, and such a pattern goes on forever (as it may be in most cases in reality), formula [5] will be adjusted and rewritten as follows:

$$V = \frac{I}{i - i\left(\dfrac{(1+g)^t - 1}{(1+i)^t - 1}\right)} \qquad [6]$$

where i is the rate of return; t is the rent review period and g is the annual growth rate.

It should be noted that in [5], i represents the rate of return or the cost of capital. But in most valuation textbooks, the Years' Purchase model of valuation method would place all risk yield in the position of i. This potential contradiction is also explained by formula [6]. When the pattern of income flow is such that it is receivable until infinity but at the same time grows progressively with time, the capitalization rate or the discount rate cannot be the rate of return if the capital value is to be ascertained from the initial income only. In this case, the interest rate employed must be able to reflect the implication of the growth potential.

Formula [6] provides such an implication in the valuation model. When the growth element is extracted from the rate of return, i, the capitalization rate becomes the all risk yield or the initial yield, k, and the relationship becomes:

$$k = i - i\left(\frac{(1+g)_t - 1}{(1+i)_t - 1}\right) \qquad [7]$$

The general model of valuation can now be established as:

$$V = \frac{I}{k} \qquad [8]$$

Hence, the capital value of a property with growth potential in rental income is the initial income divided by the all risk yield.

When applying the general model of valuation in the valuation process, there is an important underlying assumption that the investor is expecting a rate of return at least as great as i. He or she is willing to accept an all risk yield of k on the assumption that this property has a potential growth of g% p.a. such that eventually it will bring him a return of i, which is also the required investment yield. The situation can be made clear by looking at the following analogy.

If we accept that the demand for university degree courses reflects the students' future prospects (at least in most cases, except those students who enter university for the pure sake of gaining a certificate), and when such demand is quantified, it becomes the total expected future salary after graduation. Therefore the demand for certain courses (e.g. Law, Architecture, Medical Studies or Surveying) is usually higher than others. Thus if tertiary education was to be completely privatized, and school fees for different courses were to be decided by market forces, they would reflect the discounted future income of the graduates of these courses.

Bearing in mind that the future income flow would only start from the point of graduation, in times of uncertainty in the future political and economical situation, those courses with a longer course duration before income can start flowing in may find it relatively more difficult to recruit students, for the discounting effect will lower the present value of the future income flow.

In any case, the value of the courses would be equal to their price (school fees) for if the school fees are higher than the total expected income flow, and given the same academic results, students would rather choose a course that would give them a reasonable return. The increase in school fees would only be justified if there is a clear indication that the future salary would increase at a higher speed.

In choosing between courses, the starting income is not the sole consideration. For instance, a student of B.Sc. in Surveying may have a lower starting salary than a student of Education, and given the same school fees, there still might be a higher demand for the former leading to the rise in fees for the Surveying course. The reason for this does not lie with the nature of work for both professions receive reasonable social status, but with the fact that there is a higher potential growth factor in the future income in the Surveying profession. As a result students are willing to accept a lower initial yield and higher tuition fee for they perceive a higher value (hence higher rate of return) in obtaining the degree in Surveying.

It is important to understand this logical relationship between the initial all risk yield and the rate of return. The above demonstrates that there are different possible capitalization rates to be used in the valuation process. Each yield has their own underlying assumptions and limitations. It must be borne in mind that when a particular yield is to be applied, the set of assumptions that goes with it should also apply. This always creates confusion for the student for it is very easy to mix up the different yields and their assumptions. We can also use the following numerical example to further elaborate this point.

Suppose a property has a rental income per annum of HK$20. This amount is fixed and unchanged forever. Assuming rental income is receivable at the end of each year, and our required rate of return for property is 20%, we will be able to find out the value of this property by formula [3]. Since the property is for rental forever, there is no reversionary sale price and the formula [3] becomes:

$$\frac{\$20}{(1+20\%)} + \frac{\$20}{(1+20\%)^2} + \frac{\$20}{(1+20\%)^3} + \dots \frac{\$20}{(1+20\%)^{1000}} = \$100$$

[9]

Assuming year 1000 is a proxy for eternity, the summation of equation [9] is HK$100. This is obtained either through the serial calculation in equation [9] or the simplified equation [8]: HK$20/20% = HK$100. In any case, we can prove that if we pay HK$100 today, and get HK$20 per year, this is an investment with return of 20% p.a. (i.e. return or yield is equal to annual income divided by the capital value). This exactly reflects what we require before the valuation process.

Now, let us assume a more realistic situation where rental does grow as time goes by. Assuming a 12% rental growth per year due to an upsurge of demand for this kind of property,

$$\frac{\$20}{(1+20\%)} + \frac{\$22.4}{(1+20\%)^2} + \frac{\$25}{(1+20\%)^3} + \dots \frac{\$20(1+12\%)^{1000}}{(1+20\%)^{1000}} = \$250$$

[10]

If we are patient enough, we can try to add all these together and V will turn out to be HK$250. In this case, the yield has dropped to: HK$20/HK$250 = 8%! Superficially, it does not make sense. Logically, when there is an increase in demand leading to a rise in rental income, the rate of return should increase as well! In fact, the opposite happens. This is the case even when we assume that the increase in rental value starts immediately so that equation [10] becomes:

$$\frac{\$22.4}{(1+20\%)} + \frac{\$25}{(1+20\%)^2} + \frac{\$28}{(1+20\%)^3} + \cdots \frac{\$20(1+12\%)^{1000}}{(1+20\%)^{1000}} = \$280$$

[11]

In this case, V becomes HK\$280 but the yield remains 8% (i.e. HK\$22.4/HK\$280 = 0.08). The explanation to this is not at all profound. When there is future growth in the rental income, a new definition of yield is the spin off, using from the general concept of the rate of return. In fact, in both equations [10] and [11], we are not getting less than 20% p.a. This is because in both cases, we are using 20%, the required rate of return to discount future values. What is different is the initial yield we are getting. The initial income of HK\$20 or HK\$22.4 in [11] represents the initial rental level only with an implication that in the future, this level will go up at a rate of about 12% p.a. As a result, we are willing to accept a yield initially lower than we require, with the understanding that the rental income we are getting from this property will go up in the future.

Since the definition of yield is always income divided by capital value, when there is future growth in the rental level, the initial rental income is always lower than the future rental level. Hence, the initial yield will be lower than the expected rate of return. In addition, there is a hidden relationship in both equations [10] and [11]. In these two cases, we have a required rate of return of 20% p.a. and a rental growth rate of 12% p.a. When we deduct the rental growth rate from the rate of return, it becomes 8%, which is equal to the initial yield! In the later section, we will explain this relationship further. Right now, we need to amplify the point that we are willing to accept a lower than expected initial yield because we know that in the future there will be rental growth which can compensate for this gap. As a result, initial yield may be applied to future inflated income etc. There is therefore a need to have a brief discussion of these different independent variables in the valuation process.

Initial Yield or All Risk Yield

Initial yield is also commonly known as all risk yield. Fraser (1988) defines all risk yield as:

> The yield used to capitalize rent when valuing property by the Years Purchase method, being the rental income yield on rack rented freeholds and the equivalent yield on reversionary property.

Where initial yield is the initial income divided by the capital value or price of the property, all risk yield (ARY) is obtained from open market rental value and open market capital value:

$$k = \frac{\text{Current Open Market Rent}}{\text{Open Market Price or Capital Value}} \qquad [12]$$

Hence, all risk yield will only be equal to initial yield if the initial income from the property is equal to the existing open market rental value. This is the case of a property with vacant possession such that this property is ready to let at the current open market value whenever there is a prospective tenant. It should be noted that both the rental and capital values must be current open market values. Hence, the capital value of the property must be that of vacant possession and rental value must be that without premium. In this way, the ARY represents the basic risk element in the market which any average investor would expect to be compensated for in making the investment decision, which is why it is so called. (However, an investor cannot expect to be compensated for all the risks in the market).

ARY tends to be time specific in the sense that current market values change with time so that the farther away from the date of "current market value" e.g. the lease commencement date or the transaction date of the property, the less reliable the data becomes. Of course, if both rental and capital appreciate by the same magnitude, ARY tends to maintain the same level. This however, does not easily happen!

Initial yield therefore is a unique measurement of the rate of return *at* the point of valuation. It is unique in the sense that few other investment markets would measure the rate of return by looking at initial income. Moreover, rental value is very much affected by the rent review pattern. Rent for a lease with rent reviews every three years is definitely different from that with reviews every seven years, even when they are both made at the same point in time. Bowcock (1986) tackles this problem by finding the rental equivalent of tenancies with different review patterns. This however, tends to be more a mathematical exercise than an actual analysis of the market.

Expected Rate of Return

This is a general description of discount rate. In actual fact, there is a spectrum of rates to be applied. Whatever the selection is, it must be able to fulfill two basic criteria. Firstly, it must be able to match the cost of the capital. This is the minimum return required to cover at least the cost of borrowing, i.e. the interest payment on a loan. On the other hand, there is also the opportunity cost of investment capital which could have been earned at a certain rate of return from the next most profitable investment opportunity. Given similar market conditions, if these two conditions are not reflected in the expected rate of return, the investment would not be made. Within the range of different rates, investors' choices depend mainly on the risk premium associated with their attitude towards risk taking. Basically, there are the following two types of expected rates of return which provide the basic standard

Equated yield

Equated yield is the most representative rate of return in the valuation profession in the UK context. Baum and Mackmin (1989) refer to the Donaldson's Investment Tables and explain equated yield as:

> ... the discount rate which needs to be applied to the projected income so that the summation of all the incomes discounted at the expected yield rate, equates with the capital outlay....

Basically, equated yield is the internal rate of return (IRR) which the financial world has long been familiar with. It measures the true and exact return given the estimated future rental incomes. It is different from the ARY in that equated yield reflects fully the exact time preference of future money. Put in another way, it reflects the risk premium an investor would want to be compensated for, in sacrificing present consumption for future income when such income is affected only by the time factor.

However, when the equated yield is taken as the IRR, it will suffer from the same weaknesses that have occurred in the IRR (Raper, 1976).

Equity yield

On the other hand, when the economic system within which the real estate market operates fluctuates very often, it becomes relatively difficult to obtain data from the real estate market. More effort should therefore be spent on searching the money markets for information to support or adjust data obtained from the real estate market for the extraction of an appropriate rate of return. The American appraisal profession develops the equity yield which provides the relationship between the money markets and the real estate one. James E. Gibbons (1982) expresses this relationship in this way:

> ... Value has been defined as the present worth of future benefit. In real estate, this valuation concept supports the efficacy of relying on a combination of both real estate and money market analyses.... The projection of these items will best be accomplished through application of in-depth, sophisticated real estate market analysis procedures. But the rate and mathematics of discounting through which value is calculated are money matters, which are supported most effectively by capital market studies....

Gibbons also defines the equity yield as:

> ... a composite of dividend income and investment growth, or depreciation; it is usually expressed as an annual compound rate, or percentage. An equity investor has potential for upside growth and, at the same time, a substantial risk of loss flowing from the thinness of his position and its customary subordination to the requirements of operating expenses and debt service....

The assumption behind this equity yield concept is that a typical investor undertaking an investment in property would use part of his (her) own venture capital and borrow the remaining from debt sources. The combination of the proportion between these two portions varies with different investors and market conditions. In general, the higher the inflation rate, the more willing people become to borrow money rather than use their own capital. Hence, the ultimate rate of return is different under different financial assumptions.

In practice, equity yield is very similar to equated yield especially on the assumption that it represents both the elements of initial return and future growth. Nevertheless, it lends itself more to the financial analysis of the rate of return in property investment.

Rental Growth

The apparent difference in the choice of yield comes from the fact that formula [8] utilizes the market rental data at the date of valuation whereas formula [3] discounts income year by year. The relationship between the rate of return and the all risk yield therefore lies with the growth factor. In theory, rate of return is more or less the sum of the all risk yield and the growth rate. The following formula expresses this relationship:

$$\frac{1}{k} = \left(\frac{1 - PV}{i}\right) + \frac{(1 + g)_t}{k} * \frac{1}{(1 + i)_t} \qquad [13]$$

This formula provides for the link between the rate of return (i), the all risk yield (k) and the growth rate (g). It is assumed that the property produces a certain income until it is sold after year t while rental income grows at the rate of g% p.a. For the link between formulae [3] and [5] to be established, the left hand side of formula [13] must equate to the right hand side.

This formula explains the fact that formula [8] can be a good approximation of [3] **IF** the growth rate is the expected one. Hence the left hand side of [13] represents valuation by current rental value and all risk yield with rental income flowing in perpetuity. "k" is known as an implied discount rate for it incorporates the growth element in the future rental income. This implication is reflected on the right hand side of the formula. The first part on the right hand side is the capitalized rental income receivable during the holding period. After this period, the rental value is supposed to have risen to the inflated level at the growth rate. To get the capital value at that point, the inflated income $(1 + g)^{\wedge}t$ is capitalized at k but discounted for t years at i. Formula [13] in fact is also a way to find the annual growth rate, for it can be modified and transformed into the following:

$$(1 + g)^{\wedge}t = \frac{\text{YP perp. at k} - \text{YP for t years at i}}{\text{YP perp. at k} \times \text{PV for t years at i}} \qquad [14]$$

Where YP perp. is the Years Purchase formula of one dollar at a rate of k% in perpetuity, and YP for t years at i is the Years Purchase formula of one dollar at a rate of i% for t years. PV for t years at i is the Present Value of one dollar at discount rate of i% receivable after t years.

[14] can be further developed into:

$$g = i - k \qquad [15]$$

Although formulae [14] and [15] provide a way to find growth rate, it does not necessarily mean that formula [15] always represents such a logical interpretation of this relationship. This is because all risk yield k is only a capitalization rate to be applied to the current open market rental income of freehold properties with vacant possession. Although k can be found from market information (i.e. in the analysis of initial yield), it must bear the relationship between the ultimate rate of return and expected growth rate. Hence, it is more logical to interpret only i and g as independent variables. This is also why the capitalization rate in the general valuation model is called the implied initial yield. Now, let us look at some examples of the application of the investment appraisal model.

EXAMPLE 1

Advise your client on the investment value for the following real estate:

120–124, Charter Road is a 4-storey building for commercial/residential use held under single ownership by Mr Rich. Each floor has an area of 240 sq.m. The ground floor is a retail shop Me-2. The first floor is used as offices. The second floor is residential floor with two units of equal size. Mr Rich occupies the top floor.

The tenancies are as follows:

- Ground Floor:
  Retail shop held under long lease with 15 years to go at HK$650,000 p.a. with 3-yearly rent review. Current market OMR for similar shops is about HK$850,000 p.a. The next rent review is two years from now. Expected growth rate of rent is about 8% p.a. All risk yield for retail shops in the neighbourhood is about 6%.
- First floor:
  Divided into two units. Unit A (120 sq.m. in gross floor area) is occupied by a trading company with 7 years to go with no rent review at HK$350,000 p.a. Current OMR is about HK$450,000. Expected growth rate of rent is about 6% p.a. All risk yield for offices in the neighbourhood is about 8%. Unit B is currently empty (120 sq.m.) and expected to be rented out in 6 months' time.
- 2nd floor:
  Wong's Family in Flat A (120 sq.m. in gross floor area) just moved in two days ago paying HK$ 220,000 p.a. The tenancy agreement contains a normal rent review pattern. Dum's Family next door (120 sq.m. in gross floor area) has a long lease with 7 years unexpired. The lease contains no rent review. Dum's Family is now paying HK$ 135,000 p.a. Expected growth rate of rent is about 5% p.a. All risk yield for residential property in the neighbourhood is about 9%.
- 3rd floor:
  Occupied by Mr Rich.

In this example, we have both the properties with vacant possession (unit B on the first floor and the whole of third floor) and the properties with sitting tenants paying less than open market rent. When we apply investment appraisal to value this real estate, we will separate the treatment of these two kinds of interests.

First of all, from equation [8] above, we can always find the value of a property if we have the initial annual rental income and the all risk yield of this class of property. For properties with sitting tenants paying less than the market rent, the appraisal process is a little more complicated. In the British system, we have the Term and Reversion method. Under this method, we separate the rental income into term income and reversionary income. Term income refers to the income receivable during the contract term with the sitting tenant before the expiry date of the tenancy or the next rent review date. Reversionary income refers to the rental income achievable in the open market when either the occupation right reverts back to the landlord for another tenant or when the landlord is free to set a new open market rent at the rent review date. We value the interests of these two portions and add them together to get the value of the property. The only exception is Flat A of the second floor where the tenant just moved in and hence the rent the Wong's family pay to Mr Rich is the same as open market rent. Here we value the landlord's interest on the same basis as landlord's interest with vacant possession. The following solution A represents the traditional way of using the Term and Reversion method as widely adopted in the UK and to a certain extent in Hong Kong:

Solution — A: Traditional View

G/F: Term: HK$650,000 × YP @6% 2 yrs.

$$= HK\$650,000 \times \frac{1 - \dfrac{1}{(1+6\%)^2}}{6\%}$$

$$= HK\$650,000 \times 1.83$$

$$= HK\$1,189,500$$

Reversion: HK$850,000 × YP 6% in perpetuity × PV6% 2 yrs.

$$= HK\$850,000 \times \frac{1}{6\%} \times \frac{1}{(1+6\%)^2}$$

$$= HK\$850,000 \times 16.67 \times 0.89$$

$$= HK\$12,610,855$$

Value: **= HK$1,189,500 + HK$12,610,855**

= HK$13,800,355

1st/F: Unit A
Term: HK\$350,000 × YP 8% 7 yrs.

$$= HK\$350,000 \times \frac{1 - \dfrac{1}{(1 + 8\%)^7}}{8\%}$$

$$= HK\$350,000 \times 5.21$$

$$= HK\$1,823,500$$

Reversion: HK\$450,000 × YP 8% in perpetuity
× PV8% 7 yrs.

$$= HK\$450,000 \times \frac{1}{8\%} \times \frac{1}{(1 + 8\%)^7}$$

$$= HK\$450,000 \times 12.5 \times 0.58$$

$$= HK\$3,262,500$$

Value: $= \textbf{HK\$1,823,500} + \textbf{HK\$3,262,500}$

$$= \textbf{HK\$5,086,000}$$

1st/F: Unit B HK\$450,000 × YP 8% in perpetuity
× PV8% 0.5 yr

$$= HK\$450,000 \times \frac{1}{8\%} \times \frac{1}{(1 + 8\%)^{0.5}}$$

$$= HK\$450,000 \times 12.5 \times 0.962$$

Value: $= \textbf{HK\$5,411,250}$

2nd/F: Unit A HK\$220,000 × YP 9% in perpetuity

$$= HK\$220,000 \times \frac{1}{9\%}$$

$$= HK\$220,000 \times 11.11$$

Value: $= \textbf{HK\$2,444,200}$

2nd/F: Unit B
Term: HK\$135,000 × YP 9% 7 yrs.

$$= HK\$135,000 \times \frac{1 - \dfrac{1}{(1 + 9\%)^7}}{9\%}$$

$$= HK\$135,000 \times 5.033$$

$$= HK\$679,455$$

Reversion: HK$220,000 × YP 9% in perpetuity
× PV9% 7 yrs.

$$= HK\$220,000 \times \frac{1}{9\%} \times \frac{1}{(1+9\%)^7}$$

$$= HK\$220,000 \times 11.11 \times 0.55$$

$$= HK\$1,344,310$$

Value: **= HK\$1,344,310 + HK\$679,455**

= HK\$2,023,765

3rd/F: HK$440,000 × YP 9% in perpetuity

$$= HK\$440,000 \times \frac{1}{9\%}$$

$$= HK\$440,000 \times 11.11$$

Value: **= HK\$4,888,400**

Total investment value of 120–124, Charter Road is: = HK\$33,653,970

Under the traditional view using Term and Reversion method, a basic assumption is to utilize all the current market information even for future value. Hence, in the above calculations, we stick with the current open market rent when assessing the rack rent at the point of reversion. The logic behind this seemingly unreasonable assumption is that since we are using the market all risk yield to value the term portion even when there is no rent review, we will most probably over-value the term portion. In using the current open market as the rack rent at reversion, however, we will under-value this portion and hence offset the over-valuation effect in the term portion! This logic is not convincing at all, especially in the age of inflation and speculation when market rack rents may fluctuate a lot in a short period of time. As a result, we can modify this model to be more reasonable. In the following, the author will give a simplified D.C.F. approach of the Term and Reversion model based on the same example.

Solution — B: A Simplified D.C.F. Approach

G/F: Term: HK$650,000 × YP @14% 2 yrs.

$$= \text{HK\$650,000} \times \frac{1 - \dfrac{1}{(1 + 14\%)^2}}{14\%}$$

$$= \text{HK\$650,000} \times 1.65$$

$$= \text{HK\$1,072,500}$$

Reversion: HK\$850,000 $\times (1 + 8\%)^2 \times$ YP 6% in perpetuity $\times$ PV6% 2 yrs.

$$= \text{HK\$850,000} \times 1.166 \times \frac{1}{6\%} \times \frac{1}{(1 + 14\%)^2}$$

$$= \text{HK\$991,440} \times 16.67 \times 0.769$$

$$= \text{HK\$14,819,274}$$

Value: = **HK\$1,072,500** + **HK\$14,819,274**

= **HK\$15,891,774**

1st/F: Unit A

Term: HK\$350,000 $\times$ YP 14% 7 yrs.

$$= \text{HK\$350,000} \times \frac{1 - \dfrac{1}{(1 + 14\%)^7}}{14\%}$$

$$= \text{HK\$350,000} \times 4.288$$

$$= \text{HK\$1,500,907}$$

Reversion: HK\$450,000 $\times (1 + 6\%)^7$
$\times$ YP 8% in perpetuity $\times$ PV14% 7 yrs.

$$= \text{HK\$450,000} \times 1.5 \times \frac{1}{8\%} \times \frac{1}{(1 + 14\%)^7}$$

$$= \text{HK\$675,000} \times 12.5 \times 0.4$$

$$= \text{HK\$3,375,000}$$

Value: = **HK\$1,500,907** + **HK\$3,375,000**

= **HK\$4,875,907**

1st/F: Unit B HK\$450,000 $\times$ YP 8% in perpetuity
$\times$ PV8% 0.5 yr

$$= \text{HK\$450,000} \times \frac{1}{8\%} \times \frac{1}{(1 + 8\%)^{0.5}}$$

$$= \text{HK\$450,000} \times 12.5 \times 0.962$$

Value: = **HK$5,411,250**

2nd/F: Unit A   HK$220,000 × YP 9% in perpetuity

$$= \text{HK\$220,000} \times \frac{1}{9\%}$$

$$= \text{HK\$220,000} \times 11.11$$

Value: = **HK$2,444,200**

2nd/F: Unit B

Term: HK$135,000 × YP 14% 7 yrs.

$$= \text{HK\$135,000} \times \frac{1 - \dfrac{1}{(1 + 14\%)^7}}{14\%}$$

$$= \text{HK\$135,000} \times 4.288$$

$$= \text{HK\$578,880}$$

Reversion: HK$220,000 × (1 + 5%) × YP 9% in perpetuity
× PV14% 7 yrs.

$$= \text{HK\$220,000} \times 1.41 \times \frac{1}{9\%} \times \frac{1}{(1 + 14\%)^7}$$

$$= \text{HK\$310,200} \times 11.11 \times 0.4$$

$$= \text{HK\$1,378,529}$$

Value: = **HK$1,378,529 + HK$578,880**

= **HK$1,957,409**

3rd/F: HK$440,000 × YP 9% in perpetuity

$$= \text{HK\$440,000} \times \frac{1}{9\%}$$

$$= \text{HK\$440,000} \times 11.11$$

Value: = **HK$4,888,400**

Total Value: = HK$35,468,940

The main difference between this simplified D.C.F. approach and the Term and Reversion method is that the choice of the yield is in the term portion. Unlike the traditional way of valuation, this simplified D.C.F. approach considers rental income as cash flow. Hence, during the term period, rental income is fixed. When looking at the value of the term portion in the ground floor lease, for example, we are asking the following question: How much should we pay for the right to receive exactly HK$650,000 at the end of the next twelve months and another HK$650,000 at the end of another twelve months? This is a normal present value problem. Hence, we will use the discount rate to assess the present value of these two future values. The discount rate will depend on the required rate of return as this represents the opportunity cost as well as risk premium. As equation [15] has shown, we can approximate the required rate of return by adding the expected growth rate and all risk yield together. This is what we did in the calculations above.

In addition, in order to reflect the changes in the future open market rent, we will build the growth element into the future rack rent as well. As a result, in the reversionary part of the above calculations, the existing market rent is inflated at the appropriate growth rate to represent the future open market rack rent. However, in doing so we need to be very careful in the choice of the discount rate for the reversionary income. In the above simplified D.C.F. approach, we use the required rate of return to discount the reversionary open market rack rent for the assessment of its present value, since the open market rack rent at the point of reversion is the exact figure that the landlord can get at that time. Hence it is a discounting process of a future value.

If the choice of yield in the above calculations seems to be very complicated, we can remember the following rule: *The choice of yield (or discount rate) depends on the implication of the rental income*. If the rental income represents a static situation meaning the rent remains the same through the prescribed period, then the required rate of return should be used for both the PV formula and the YP formula. If however the rental income represents the initial level only and there is an expectation that this rental level will change in the future (normally upward movement), we should use the all risk yield in the discounting process. This is because all risk yield implies that there is future growth in the rental income (equation [15]). Mathematically, all risk yield is smaller than the required rate of return and this smaller discount rate will give a larger YP figure.

If readers accept that this simplified D.C.F. approach to the valuation model represents a more reasonable and realistic view of the real estate value, then we can further develop this simplified D.C.F. approach into a better-structured valuation model. This is the Discounted Cash Flow model, more commonly known as the D.C.F. model. The following example can demonstrate the effectiveness of this model.

EXAMPLE 2

Suppose there is an office unit with a sitting tenant paying HK$200 p.a. as rent when the current open market is HK$400 p.a. We want to know how much a prospective investor should pay for this real estate by the D.C.F. model.

From the table of Example 2, we know that this property is worth HK$4,256. Column 1 of the model represents the length of each valuation period. As we assume that the normal market rent review pattern is every three years, we are getting a fixed income every three years. Column 2 shows the rental income receivable at the beginning of the valuation period. Column 3 is for the expenses which we may like to fill in if there are regular expenses for this property (see the next example). Hence, Column 4 is the net income after deduction of expenses. Column 5 is the YP factor (at a discount rate of 14%, the required rate of return). It remains the same figure until after year 75 because every valuation period has the same length (three years). At the beginning of year 76, because we want to simplify the calculation into eternity, we assess the capital value of the property at that point of time by the traditional way of dividing the rental value by the all risk yield. Since we are not forecasting future income anymore, the use of all risk yield for this initial income at year 76 (HK$30,955) is justified. Column 6 is the PV factor to bring the various future values back to the same basis, i.e. present value. Finally, the last column is Column 6 multiplied by Column 5 making the present value of rental incomes receivable at each valuation period. The summation of all these present values together will give us the value of this property.

We can see from this example the versatility of the D.C.F. model. The biggest advantage of this model over the traditional one is the capacity to allow for variations in cash flow patterns

Example 2 office property renting at HK$200 per year (signed under a long lease in the past), with 3 years unexpired. Current Open Market Rent (OMR) is HK$400

rental expected to grow at 6% p.a.

expected rate of return: 14% p.a.

Discounted Cash Flow (D.C.F.) Analysis:

1	2	3	4	5	6	7
Year	Rental	Expenses	Net Income	YP	P.V.	Total
1–3	$200	$0	$200	2.321632	1.00000	$464
4–6	$476	$0	$476	2.321632	0.67497	$746
7–9	$566	$0	$566	2.321632	0.45559	$599
10–12	$674	$0	$674	2.321632	0.30751	$481
13–15	$802	$0	$802	2.321632	0.20756	$387
16–18	$955	$0	$955	2.321632	0.14010	$310
19–21	$1,136	$0	$1,136	2.321632	0.09456	$249
22–24	$1,352	$0	$1,352	2.321632	0.06383	$200
25–27	$1,609	$0	$1,609	2.321632	0.04308	$161
28–30	$1,914	$0	$1,914	2.321632	0.02908	$129
31–33	$2,278	$0	$2,278	2.321632	0.01963	$104
34–36	$2,711	$0	$2,711	2.321632	0.01325	$83
37–39	$3,226	$0	$3,226	2.321632	0.00894	$67
40–42	$3,839	$0	$3,839	2.321632	0.00604	$54
43–45	$4,568	$0	$4,568	2.321632	0.00407	$43
46–48	$5,436	$0	$5,436	2.321632	0.00275	$35
49–51	$6,469	$0	$6,469	2.321632	0.00186	$28
52–54	$7,698	$0	$7,698	2.321632	0.00125	$22
55–57	$9,160	$0	$9,160	2.321632	0.00085	$18
58–60	$10,901	$0	$10,901	2.321632	0.00057	$14
61–63	$12,972	$0	$12,972	2.321632	0.00039	$12
64–66	$15,436	$0	$15,436	2.321632	0.00026	$9
67–69	$18,369	$0	$18,369	2.321632	0.00018	$7
70–72	$21,859	$0	$21,589	2.321632	0.00012	$6
73–75	$26,013	$0	$26,013	2.321632	0.00008	$5
76+	$30,955	$0	$30,955	2.321632	0.00005	$21
					Total Value:	$4,256

during the holding period of the real estate. The following example 3, shows the capacity of the D.C.F. model to incorporate two major changes in the cash flow pattern of the real estate. One is the annual expenses allowing for annual inflation growth.

The other is the change in the future growth rate of the rental income (which in actual cases can be positive or negative):

EXAMPLE 3

Example 3 office property renting at HK$1,080,000 per year (2000 sq. ft.) (or HK$45/sq. ft./month) rental expected to grow at 8% p.a. until six years later at 12% p.a.
Inflation: 10% p.a.
expected rate of return: 0.14
What is the Value of this property?
Discounted Cash Flow (D.C.F.) Analysis:

Year	Rental	Expenses	Net Income	YP	P.V.	Total
1	$1,080,000	$200,000	$880,000	1	0.87719	$771,930
2	$1,080,000	$220,000	$860,000	1	0.76947	$661,742
3	$1,080,000	$242,000	$838,000	1	0.67497	$565,626
4	$1,359,720	$266,200	$1,093,520	1	0.59208	$647,452
5	$1,359,720	$292,820	$1,066,900	1	0.51937	$554,114
6	$1,359,720	$322,102	$1,037,618	1	0.45559	$472,725
7	$1,712,839	$354,312	$1,358,527	1	0.39964	$542,918
8	$1,712,839	$389,743	$1,323,096	1	0.35056	$463,823
9	$1,712,839	$428,718	$1,284,122	1	0.30751	$394,878
10	$2,406,368	$471,590	$1,934,778	1	0.26974	$521,894
11	$2,406,368	$518,748	$1,887,619	1	0.23662	$446,644
12	$2,406,368	$570,623	$1,835,745	1	0.20756	$381,025
13	$3,380,706	$627,686	$2,753,021	1	0.18207	$501,241
14	$3,380,706	$690,454	$2,690,252	1	0.15971	$429,660
15	$3,380,706	$759,500	$2,621,207	1	0.14010	$367,222
16	$4,749,554	$835,450	$3,914,105	1	0.12289	$481,011
17	$4,749,554	$918,995	$3,830,560	1	0.10780	$412,933
18	$4,749,554	$1,010,894	$3,738,660	1	0.09456	$353,532
19	$6,672,649	$1,111,983	$5,560,665	1	0.08295	$461,248
20	$6,672,649	$1,223,182	$5,449,467	1	0.07276	$396,513
21	$6,672,649	$1,345,500	$5,327,149	1	0.06383	$340,011
22	$9,374,404	$1,480,050	$7,894,354	1	0.05599	$441,987
23	$9,374,404	$1,628,055	$7,746,349	1	0.04911	$380,439
24	$9,374,404	$1,790,860	$7,583,544	1	0.04308	$326,705
25	$13,170,101	$1,969,947	$11,200,154	1	0.03779	$423,256
26	$13,170,101	$2,166,941	$11,003,159	1	0.03315	$364,747
27	$13,170,101	$2,383,635	$10,786,465	1	0.02908	$313,652

Example 3 (Cont'd)

Year	Rental	Expenses	Net Income	YP	P.V.	Total
28	$18,502,674	$2,621,999	$15,880,675	1	0.02551	$405,073
29	$18,502,674	$2,884,199	$15,618,476	1	0.02237	$349,460
30	$18,502,674	$3,172,619	$15,330,056	1	0.01963	$300,883
31	$25,994,407	$3,489,880	$22,504,527	1	0.01722	$387,453
32	$25,994,407	$3,838,868	$22,155,539	1	0.01510	$334,601
33	$25,994,407	$4,222,755	$21,771,652	1	0.01325	$288,424
34	$36,519,542	$4,645,031	$31,874,512	1	0.01162	$370,406
35	$36,519,542	$5,109,534	$31,410,008	1	0.01019	$320,183
36	$36,519,542	$5,620,487	$30,899,055	1	0.00894	$276,293
37	$51,306,305	$6,182,536	$45,123,769	1	0.00784	$353,937
38	$51,306,305	$6,800,790	$44,505,515	1	0.00688	$306,217
39	$51,306,305	$7,480,869	$43,825,436	1	0.00604	$264,507
40	$72,080,228	$8,228,956	$63,851,273	1	0.00529	$338,046
41	$72,080,228	$9,051,851	$63,028,377	1	0.00464	$292,710
42	$72,080,228	$9,957,036	$62,123,192	1	0.00407	$253,075
43	$101,265,512	$10,952,740	$90,312,773	1	0.00357	$322,731
44	$101,265,512	$12,048,014	$89,217,499	1	0.00313	$279,664
45	$101,265,512	$13,252,815	$88,012,697	1	0.00275	$242,006
46	$142,267,919	$14,578,097	$127,689,822	1	0.00241	$307,988
47	$142,267,919	$16,035,906	$126,232,012	1	0.00212	$267,080
48	$142,267,919	$17,639,497	$124,628,421	1	0.00186	$231,305
49	$199,872,199	$19,403,447	$180,468,752	1	0.00163	$293,808
50	$199,872,199	$21,343,791	$178,528,407	1	0.00143	$254,956
51	$199,872,199	$23,478,171	$176,394,028	1	0.00125	$220,972
52	$280,800,452	$25,825,988	$254,974,464	1	0.00110	$280,185
53	$280,800,452	$28,408,586	$252,391,866	1	0.00096	$243,287
54	$280,800,452	$31,249,445	$249,551,007	1	0.00085	$211,007
55	$394,496,555	$34,374,390	$360,122,165	1	0.00074	$267,106
56	$394,496,555	$37,811,828	$356,684,726	1	0.00065	$232,067
57	$394,496,555	$41,593,011	$352,903,544	1	0.00057	$201,409
58	$554,228,210	$45,752,312	$508,475,898	1	0.00050	$254,559
59	$554,228,210	$50,327,544	$503,900,666	1	0.00044	$221,288
60	$554,228,210	$55,360,298	$498,867,912	1	0.00039	$192,174
61	$778,635,212	$60,896,328	$717,738,884	1	0.00034	$242,533
62	$778,635,212	$66,985,961	$711,649,252	1	0.00030	$210,943
63	$778,635,212	$73,684,557	$704,950,656	1	0.00026	$183,296
64	$1,093,904,610	$81,053,012	$1,012,851,597	1	0.00023	$231,012
65	$1,093,904,610	$89,158,314	$1,004,746,296	1	0.00020	$201,021
66	$1,093,904,610	$98,074,145	$995,830,465	1	0.00018	$174,769
67	$1,536,826,586	$107,881,560	$1,428,945,027	1	0.00015	$219,984
68	$1,536,826,586	$118,669,716	$1,418,156,871	1	0.00014	$191,511

Example 3 (Cont'd)

Year	Rental	Expenses	Net Income	YP	P.V.	Total
69	$1,536,826,586	$130,536,687	$1,406,289,899	1	0.00012	$166,587
70	$2,159,087,671	$143,590,356	$2,015,497,315	1	0.00010	$209,432
71	$2,159,087,671	$157,949,391	$2,001,138,280	1	0.00009	$182,403
72	$2,159,087,671	$173,744,330	$1,985,343,341	1	0.00008	$158,740
73	$3,033,302,269	$191,118,764	$2,842,183,506	1	0.00007	$199,342
74	$3,033,302,269	$210,230,640	$2,823,071,629	1	0.00006	$173,685
75	$3,033,302,269	$231,253,704	$2,802,048,565	1	0.00005	$151,221
76	$4,261,486,358	$254,379,074	$4,007,107,284	1	0.00005	$189,698
77	$4,261,486,358	$279,816,982	$3,981,669,376	1	0.00004	$165,345
78	$4,261,486,358	$307,798,680	$3,953,687,678	1	0.00004	$144,020
79	$5,986,962,184	$338,578,548	$5,648,383,636	1	0.00003	$180,485
80	$5,986,962,184	$372,436,403	$5,614,525,782	1	0.00003	$157,371
81	$5,986,962,184	$409,680,043	$5,577,282,141	1	0.00002	$137,129
82	$8,411,083,173	$450,648,047	$7,960,435,125	1	0.00002	$171,688
83	$8,411,083,173	$495,712,852	$7,915,370,321	1	0.00002	$149,751
84	$8,411,083,173	$545,284,137	$7,865,799,035	1	0.00002	$130,538
85+	$11,816,730,749	$599,812,551	$11,216,918,19	12.5	0.00001	$2,041,133

Total Value: $28,147,424

Typical distinction between traditional UK approach and D.C.F. model:

EXAMPLE 4

Prime office building investment
Investment appraisal based on D.C.F.

Data: office GFA: 212500 sf.ft.   (8500 sq.ft./floor, and 25 storey high)
OMR: $75.00 psf/month
contract rent $55.00 psf/month
expected holding period: 5 years
expected rate of return: 15%
market yield: 8%
expected growth rate: 7% p.a.
management cost: 4.5 psf/month   (rises by 8% p.a.)
next rent review: 2 years later
market rent review pattern 3-yearly

Example 4 (Cont'd)

Prime office building investment
Investment appraisal based on D.C.F.

D.C.F. analysis:

Year	Rental	Cost	Net Income	PV factor @15%	PV
1	$140,250,000.0	$11,475,000.0	$128,775,000.0	0.869565	$111,978,260.9
2	$140,250,000.0	$12,393,000.0	$127,857,000.0	0.756144	$96,678,260.9
3	$218,962,125.0	$13,384,440.0	$205,577,685.0	0.657516	$135,170,664.9
4	$218,962,125.0	$14,455,195.2	$204,506,929.8	0.571753	$116,927,500.9
5	$218,962,125.0	$15,611,610.8	$203,350,514.2	0.497177	$101,101,144.8
6*	$268,238,018.5	$16,860,539.7	$251,377,478.8	6.214709	$1,562,237,928.1
				Total:	$2,124,093,760.3

*:   sale price at the beginning of year 6 is equal to:
OMR at year 6 divided by market yield (assumed to be 8% as well)
but discounted for FIVE years hence: $251,377,478.8 ×
(1/0.08 × 0.497177) = $1,562,237,928.1

Compared this with traditional approach of Term and Reversion:

Term income:	$140,250,000.0 × YP @8% 2 years	=	$ 250,107,825.0
Reversion:	$191,250,000.0 × YP @8%, PV 2 years		$2,049,568,875.0
		Total:	$2,299,676,700.0

EXAMPLE 5

The following example is constructed in order to further demonstrate the rationality of the investment appraisal approach in
assessing asset value and the difference between this investment
appraisal based on cash flow analysis and the traditional simple
valuation approach. Example 5 below, is an investment opportunity for a grade B, or secondary office building 13 floors high.
Each floor has a gross floor area of 10,000 square feet. The current
owner is asking for HK$500 million. The current annual operating
expenses of the landlord are about HK260,000 with an expected
growth rate of 10%. If a prospective purchaser is expecting to
hold the property for 5 years with a plan to sell it at the beginning
of year 6, and his expected rate of return is 12% p.a., would it
be a good investment? First of all, before a cash flow analysis
can be conducted, one will need to look at the current tenancy

profile to estimate the future cash flow pattern for this investment appraisal. The following shows the current tenancy profile:

Tenants' Profile:

Floor	Area (sq.ft.)	Tenant	Rent paying p.a.	Remarks
1–3 floors	30,000	Pacific Group	$2,600,000	lease will expire next year. Due to the size of this tenancy, normally a 15% discount on OMR will be given to the tenant, who has indicated interest in staying.
4/F Unit A	5,000	Vacant	$—	
4/F Unit B	2,500	Lotus (HK)	$125,000	just moved in for a standard 3-year lease
4/F Unit C	2,500	Vacant	$—	
5–6/F	20,000	HK Wonders	$10,080,000	lease due to review in 2 years' time with a further 3 years after review. Due to the size of this tenancy, normally a 10% discount on OMR will be given.
7/F Unit A	6,500	Cashworld Ltd.	$3,432,000	lease due to review in 2 years' time with a further 3 years after rent review.
7/F Unit B	3,500	Skywalker Ltd.	$2,226,000	lease due to expire in 2 years, tenant has strong intention to relocate
8–10/F (Unit A)	25,000	Solitaire & Partners	$9,900,000	lease due to expire in 2 years, tenant has indicated that they would like to reduce the space they rent to 9000 sq.ft.
10/F Unit B	5,000	Vacant	$—	
11/F	10,000	Vacant	$—	
12/F	10,000	Sino Hong Co.	$4,800,000	lease due to expire in 2 years' time.
13/F	10,000	Vacant	$—	
Occupancy:	97,500	75%	$43,163,000	Annual Rental Income

Given that the objective of this investor is to hold the property for five years and to enjoy the income and possible capital gains after five years, there will be a need to estimate of the occupancy, as well as market conditions in this sector of the market, for the assessment of income flows. Now, let us assume that the market is not particularly promising in the coming two years. It is expected that rent will fall by 6 percent p.a. in the coming two years, but will climb up again at 12% p.a. after that. Moreover, the occupancy rate for this building, after researching possible supply in the market and talking to existing tenants is estimated to be as follows:

coming two years   : 75%
Year 3   : 60%
Year 4   : 70%
Year 5 and beyond : 75%

In addition, it is also established by the investor that the disposal capitalization rate at the beginning of year 6 will be 8%. Having established all this, the next step is to estimate the cash flow pattern during the holding period. Rental income receivable this year can be calculated based on the existing tenancy profile. Future income can be estimated based on expected occupancy rate as follows:

Annual Analysis:	Yr. 2	Open Market Rent:	$47 /sq.ft/month	
Floor:	Area (sq.ft.)	Tenant	Rent paying p.a.	Remarks
1–3 floors	30,000	Pacific Group	$14,382,000	new lease for three years with 15% discount on OMR
4/F Unit A	5,000	Vacant	$—	
4/F Unit B	2,500	Lotus (HK)	$125,000	second year occupation
4/F Unit C	2,500	Vacant	$—	
5–6/F	20,000	HK Wonders	$10,080,000	lease review in 1 years' time with a further 3 years after review

(Cont'd)

Annual Analysis:	Yr. 2	Open Market Rent:	$47 /sq.ft/month	
Floor:	Area (sq.ft.)	Tenant	Rent paying p.a.	Remarks
7/F Unit A	6,500	Cashworld Ltd.	$3,432,000	lease review in 1 years' time with a further 3 years after review
7/F Unit B	3,500	Skywalker Ltd.	$2,226,000	lease due to expire in 1 year, tenant has strong intention to relocate
8–10/F (Unit A)	25,000	Solitaire & Partners	$9,900,000	lease will expire next year, tenant has indicated that they would reduce space to 9000 sq.ft.
10/F Unit B	5,000	Vacant	$—	
11/F	10,000	Vacant	$—	
12/F	10,000	Sino Hong Co.	$4,800,000	lease due to expire in 1 years' time
13/F	10,000	Vacant	$—	
Occupancy:	97,500	75%	$44,945,000	Annual Rental Income

Annual Analysis:	Yr. 3	Market Rent:	$50 /sq.ft./month	
Floor:	Area (sq.ft.)	Tenant	Rent paying p.a.	Remarks
1–3 floors	30,000	Pacific Group	$4,382,000	second year occupation
4/F Unit A	5,000	Vacant	$—	
4/F Unit B	2,500	Lotus (HK)	$125,000	final year occupation
$/F Unit C	2,500	Vacant	$—	
5–6/F	20,000	HK Wonders	$9,745,920	new rent at review
7/F Unit A	6,500	Cashworld	$3,519,360	new rent at review
7/F Unit B	3,500	vacant	$—	
8/F Unit A	3,000	vacant	$—	

(Cont'd)

Annual Analysis: Floor:	Yr. 3 Area (sq.ft.)	Market Rent: Tenant	$50 /sq.ft./month Rent paying p.a.	Remarks
8/F Unit B–9/F Unit A	9,000	Solitaire & Partners	$4,872,960	new lease with smaller office
9/F B–10/F	18,000	Vacant	$—	
11/F	10,000	Vacant	$—	
12/F	10,000	Sino Hong Co.	$5,414,400	new 3 year lease
13/F	10,000	Vacant	$—	
Occupancy:	78,000	60%	$38,059,640	Annual Rental Income

Annual Analysis: Floor:	Yr. 4 Area (sq.ft.)	Market Rent: Tenant	$50 /sq.ft./month Rent paying p.a.	Remarks
1–3 floors	30,000	Pacific Group	$14,382,000	final year
4/F Unit A	5,000	Vacant	$—	
4/F Unit B	2,500	Lotus (HK)	$126,000	new lease
4/F Unit C	2,500	Vacant	$—	
5–6/F	20,000	HK Wonders	$10,886,400	second year
7/F Unit A	6,500	Cashworld	$3,931,200	second year
7/F Unit B	3,500	vacant	$—	
8/F Unit A	3,000	Vacant	$—	
8/F Unita A–9/F Unit A	9,000	Solitaire & Partners	$5,443,200	second year
9/F B–10/F A	13,000	Vacant	$—	
10/F Unit B	5,000	Big Deal Ltd.	$3,024,000	new 3 year lease
11/F Unit A	5,000	New Agency	$3,024,000	new 3 year lease
11/F Unit B	5,000	Vacant	$—	

(Cont'd)

Annual Analysis: Floor:	Yr. 4 Area (sq.ft.)	Market Rent: Tenant	$50 /sq.ft./month Rent paying p.a.	Remarks
12/F	10,000	Sino Hong Co.	$6,048,000	second year
13/F Unit A	3,000	I.O.U. Ltd.	$1,814,400	new 3 year lease
13/F Unit B	7,000	Vacant	$—	
Occupancy:	91,000	70%	$48,679,200	Annual Rental Income

Annual Analysis: Floor:	Yr. 5 Area (sq.ft.)	Market Rent: Tenant	$56 /sq.ft./month Rent paying p.a.	Remarks
1–3 floors	30,000	Pacific Group	$17,273,088	new lease (with 15% discount)
4/F Unit A	5,000	Vacant	$—	
4/F Unit B	2,500	Lotus (HK)	$126,000	second year
4/F Unit C	2,500	Vacant	$—	
5–6/F	20,000	HK Wonders	$10,886,400	final year
7/F Unit A	6,500	Cashworld	$3,931,200	final year
7/F Unit B– 8/F Unit A	6,500	New Union Ltd.	$4,402,944	new 3 year lease
8/F Unit B– 9/F Unit A	9,000	Solitaire & Partners	$5,443,200	final year
9/F B–10/F A	13,000	Vacant	$—	
10/F Unit B	5,000	Big Deal Ltd.	$3,024,000	second year
11/F Unit A	5,000	New Agency	$3,024,000	second year
11/F Unit B	5,000	Vacant	$—	
12/F	10,000	Sino Hong Co.	$6,048,000	final year
13/F Unit A	3,000	I.O.U. Ltd.	$1,814,400	second year
13/F Unit B	7,000	Vacant	$—	
Occupancy:	97,500	75%	$55,988,352	Annual Rental Income

The above shows the expected income flow during the holding period of five years. In principle, the value of this property is the sum of discounted values of these five years' incomes plus the discounted disposal value of the whole building at the beginning of year 6. Given the above estimation of the five years' income flow and the expected rate of return of 12% as discount rate, there should not be any problem in finding the total present values of this income. The major problem in this investment appraisal lies with the estimation of the disposal value. In arriving at this value, there is a need to predict the tenancy profile at the beginning of year 6.

Floor	Yr. 6 Area (sq.ft.)	Market Rent: Tenant	$63 /sq.ft./month Rent paying p.a.	Remarks
1–3	30,000	Pacific Group	$17,273,088	second year
4/F Unit A	5,000	Vacant	$—	
4/F Unit B	2,500	Lotus (HK)	$126,000	final year
4/F Unit C	2,500	Vacant	$—	
5–6/F	20,000	HK Wonders	$13,655,900	new lease
7/F Unit A	6,500	Cashworld Ltd.	$4,931,297	new lease
7/F B–8/F A	6,500	New Union Ltd.	$4,402,944	second year
8/F B–9/F A	9,000	Solitaire & Partners	$6,827,950	new lease
9/F B–10/F A	13,000	Vacant	$—	
10/F Unit B	5,000	Big Deal Ltd.	$3,024,000	final year
11/F Unit A	5,000	New Agency Co.	$3,024,000	final year
11/F Unit B	5,000	Vacant	$—	
12/F	10,000	Sino Hong Co.	$7,586,611	new lease
13/F Unit A	3,000	I.O.U. Ltd.	$1,814,400	final year
13/F Unit B	7,000	Vacant	$—	
	97,500	75%	$62,681,311	Annual Rental Income

Future Rental Analysis:

new lease:	$33,001,759	45,500 sq.ft.
second year:	$21,676,032	36,500 sq.ft.
final year:	$ 7,988,400	15,500 sq.ft.

The purpose of setting the tenancy profile at the beginning of year 6 is that if the investor is going to sell this building at the beginning of year 6 after enjoying five years incomes, he should expect the new purchaser to do exactly what he did five years ago, i.e. estimate the cash flow patterns after the transfer of ownership. Transfer of ownership begins with year 6. The new purchaser, knowing that he will be bound by some existing leases with a rental payment lower than the current open market rent in year 6, will not apply formula [5] described above in assessing the value of the office building. Hence, he will not be expecting to pay a price which represents the open market value of the building in year 6 divided by the capitalization rate of 8%.

On the other hand, it will not be realistic for this investor to estimate the changes in the cash flow patterns forever from the view point of the new purchaser. Since formula [5] is the hard-core of the value of any income-producing asset, this formula will still be utilized, but in a slightly different way.

A practical way of making the investment appraisal in this case for the assessment of the value of this office building will therefore be similar to the traditional term and reversion approach described above. In the term portion, the value is equal to the discounted values of the five years' incomes. In the reversion portion, instead of estimating the open market rent for the whole building as in both the traditional view or the simplified D.C.F. approach, those leases with a rental level below the year 6 open market rent will be discounted back to the point as at the beginning of year 6. The reason for discounting to the beginning of year 6 first instead of afterwards will be explained later. This is expressed more clearly by Figure 18.

But now, if we look at the tenancy profile of year 6, we will find that at the bottom of the table, there is a future rental analysis. Basically it is the summary of how many leases (in terms of rental value) are let at the current (year 6) open market rent, how many were signed two years ago so that the new purchaser will still be bound by them for one more year, and how many the new purchaser will still have to honour for two more years before he can revise them to the open market rent.

From the future rental analysis in the above example can be seen that a value of about $33 million worth of leases could be

Figure 18 The Reason for Discounting

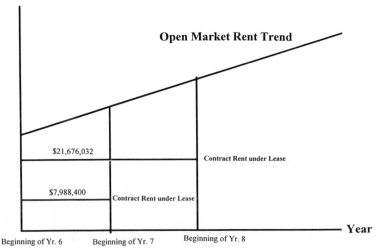

Point of Disposal

Open Market Rent Trend

$21,676,032

Contract Rent under Lease

$7,988,400

Contract Rent under Lease

Year

Beginning of Yr. 6   Beginning of Yr. 7   Beginning of Yr. 8

let at year 6 open market rent. As they are open market value, the capital value of this portion can be found by dividing this open market rental value (less annual operating expenses at the beginning of year 6) by the capitalization rate of 8%:

$$\frac{(\$33,001,759 - \$418,733)}{8\%} = \$407,287,825 \text{ (valued as at the beginning of year 6)}$$

The next portion is the value of the leases with one year to expiry or review to open market level. The contract rental value of this portion by the end of year 6 is $ 7,988,400. This amount will be discounted at 12% for one year after allowing the appropriate annual operating expenses (i.e. $\frac{\$7,988,400 - \$418,733}{1 + 12\%} =$ $6,758,631.25). Upon renewal or review of these leases, open market rent will be required by the new purchaser at the level of HK$63 × 1.12 (12% being the expected annual growth rate of rent as assumed in the beginning). Since it is assumed that occupancy rate remains at 75% after year 5, there will be no changes in the space occupied, or in the tenancy profile. The new rental income (open market level) receivable from these lease will be (at the beginning of year 7):

15,500 sq.ft. × HK\$63(1.12) × 12 months = HK\$13,124,160 p.a. To arrive at the net income figure, the annual operating expenses in year 7 will be deducted making the net figure as: HK\$12,663,553.7 p.a. At this point, since it is an open market rent figure, formula [5] can be applied to find the capital value figure at the beginning of year 6 (together with a present value formula at 12%):

$$\frac{\$12,663,533.7}{8\%} \times \frac{1}{(1+12\%)} = \$141,334,304.7 \text{ (valued as at the beginning of year 6)}$$

Hence, the total value for this portion is: HK\$141,334,304.7 + HK\$6,758,631.25 = HK\$148,092,936.95

Finally, the last portion in the disposal value will be the value of those leases with two more years to run at less than open market rent. The annual value of these leases is HK\$21,676,032 with a total area of 36,500 sq.ft. Based on the logic above, the total discounted value of the contractual value is:

$$\frac{\$2,167,032 - \$418,733}{(1+12\%)} + \frac{\$2,167,032 - \$468,981}{(1+12\%)^2} = \$35,885,862.5$$

(valued as at the beginning of year 6). Similarly, the open market value for this building at the beginning of year 8, i.e. when these leases will be renewed or reviewed is \$63 × $(1.12)^2$ = \$79/sq.ft/month. The capital value of these leases at the point of renewal of leases or review date is:

$$\frac{\$34,602,000}{8\%} \times \frac{1}{(1+12\%)^2} = \$344,806,282 \text{ (valued as at the beginning of year 6).}$$

The total value of the leases for this portion at the beginning of year 6 is:

\$35,885,862.5 + \$344,806,282 = \$380,692,144.5

Therefore, the disposal value at the beginning of year 6, or the acceptable price from the new purchaser at the beginning of year 6 after the holding period is: \$407,287,825 + \$148,092,936.95 + \$380,692,144.5 = \$936,072,905.4 (valued at the beginning of year 6). Now, we should explain why we only discount these values to the beginning of year 6. Since transaction cost will be incurred (such as stamp duty and legal charges), a 3% transaction cost must be deducted from this disposal value before discounting back to the present time. Hence, the disposal value at today's value is:

$$\frac{\$936,086,405.4 \times (1 - 3\%)}{(1 + 12\%)^5} = \$515,218,317.2 \text{ (as at today's value)}$$

When all the discounted values of the income flow during the holding period are added together with this figure, it becomes the investment value of this office building as demonstrated below:

Discounted Cash Flow (D.C.F.) Analysis:

Year	Rental income	Expenses	Net Income	YP	P.V.	Total
1	$43,163,000	$260,000	$42,903,000	1	0.89286	$23,306,250*
2	$44,945,000	$286,000	$44,659,000	1	0.79719	$35,601,881
3	$38,059,640	$314,600	$37,745,040	1	0.71178	$26,866,174
4	$48,679,200	$346,060	$48,333,140	1	0.63552	$30,716,584
5	$55,988,352	$380,666	$55,607,686	1	0.56743	$31,553,294
		$418,733		12.5		$515,225,748.5#
			Total Discounted Value:			$663,269,931.5
					NPV:	$163,269,931.5

*: Transaction cost of 3% on asking price is deducted.
#: HK$33001759 × YP of 12.5 plus discounted values of continuing leases minus transaction cost of 3%.

This may produce a big contrast with the traditional term and reversion valuation model where only the current market data is being utilized. Under such a traditional model, the value of this building will simply be the term income (which is the initial income at the beginning of the holding period) multiplied by the Y.P. factor:

$$\$43,163,000 \times \frac{1 - \frac{1}{(1 + i\%)^5}}{i\%}$$

plus the reversion value based on open market rent today as an estimation of the open market in five years' time:

$$\$78,000,000 \times \frac{1}{i\%} \times \frac{1}{(1 + i\%)^5}$$

Where i% is relevant capitalization rate at the current market situation. Without the appropriate current capitalization rate, it will be difficult to compare the merits of the two models. However, if a rational investor looks at this particular investment opportunity with a similar plan of holding it for five years and then reselling it to some other investor, there is no reason why a cash flow approach will not suit his own financial planning. Moreover, any reasonable prospective purchaser in year 6 will do exactly the same as the investor by looking at the cash flow pattern of the building before setting a price for the premises. In this way, investment appraisal as opposed to the traditional valuation model can not only provide an answer to the search for a value figure but also provide an important tool for the financial consideration of the investor. In this way, the role of appraisal will be greatly enhanced beyond just a mechanism for "guessing price."

Summary

Appraisal addresses the principle. The valuation method is concerned with practice. As seen in the previous sections, each method puts emphasis on different aspects of the market variables. Each has their own set of assumptions under which the technique operates. In theory, market comparison is the most representative method for this shows exactly what is happening in the market and how people react to different information, provided that, of course, the market is operating efficiently. This does not always happen.

Moreover, price is always a historical figure. It is only created after a market transaction has taken place. Value on the other hand is a forward looking element. It shows how the property asset will benefit the owner in the future holding period in both utility terms and monetary terms. Under this concept, the income approach or investment method seems to be more appropriate in explaining the value element.

It may be argued that the property owner is only interested

in the probable selling price. If the market is accepting a certain price level as the clearing price, the personal considerations of the individual investor do not matter. Fraser (1988) elaborates this argument by making an analogy from the stock market that:

> ... Before making a buy/sell/hold recommendation, a stockbroker's analyst will undertake a fundamental analysis. He will investigate the likely future earnings ... he will make a judgment about the inherent worth of the shares ... if a client wishes to know the market value of his shares, the broker will not undertake any analysis, but will call up the appropriate page on computer screen showing current price....

In actual fact, market comparison and the investment approach should not preclude one another. The investment method of valuation does not consider and analyse the individual investment position only. A lot of elements in the valuation process are in fact market data such as growth expectation, rental data and market yield. Therefore incorporating analysis into the valuation does not cause it to deviate from the market concept, but instead provides the missing link for the various elements in the market.

In addition, it would make property more capable of comparison with other investment vehicles for it provides enough data for investor's considerations. Moreover, because of the lack of capital funds in general, real property is not traded as frequent as we usually experience in the free market economy. Real estate development therefore normally takes the form of investment so that investment criteria in the valuation process becomes very important.

Appraisal is not about the mathematical process through which a statistically precise figure can be created and proven. It is about the explanation of the interrelationship between the different variables in the real estate market from the micro level and in the economy from the macro level. Without such an understanding, the application of valuation is very restrictive. Brown (1991) remarks that:

> ... the correct role of valuation models is to define the economic relationship between the relevant variables in order to arrive at values which could establish a market in equilibrium.... The principle function of valuation models in this context therefore is to establish whether

individual properties offered for sale are either under- or over-priced relative to their equilibrium market values ... valuation is drafted in terms of expectations and is a reflection on the quality and the amount of information....

As concluded in the previous chapter, the investment approach to valuation provides a relatively economic logic explaining the composition of capital value. The general valuation model as outlined above is very often taken for granted. There is a need to understand the difference between the implied discount rate and the rate of return, for they apply to different sets of assumptions, especially about rental growth. There are advantages and weaknesses in the application of either rate. The most important thing is that their assumptions should not be mixed.

The general valuation model is very simple and straightforward. However, there are some variables to be examined and defined before proper valuation can be carried out. To achieve this effectively, more information is needed not only from the real estate market, but from other financial markets. Gibbons (1982) summarizes the role of surveyors (appraisers) in the following words:

> ... It is noted that many real estate appraisers are uncomfortable about relying on securities analysts for projections of future dividend income and stock price growth and depreciation. This function, however, is an essential ingredient in all valuations.... In the real estate field, it is the appraisers who develops forecasts of future earnings and prices; in the securities field, the securities analyst performs the same function.... In any event, with the type of combined real estate and stock market studies described, ... real estate appraisers and investment analysts would surely be better prepared to develop persuasive valuations and effectively counsel clients in difficult investment decisions. Above all, the appraisal profession should have a clear view of the nature of equity yield and more available, objective evidence to support the rate selection....

It seems fairly clear that the general valuation model provides only a quick guide to capital value IF the market situation is reasonably rational. This does not always apply. This is especially true when property investment is no longer taken as an individual investment decision, but as one of the decisions in a bigger basket of various investment opportunities. This does not apply only to giant investors, but also to average investors. As the information flow between different markets becomes more efficient, investors are more concerned with the real rate of return that can be earned given the various opportunities. More accurate valuations are required to satisfy such a situation.

Moreover, relying solely on the general model will not allow the surveyor to reveal the underlying economic assumptions and the interrelationship between variables. If the relationship between the required rate of return and the all risk yield is not understood, the growth element cannot be elaborated. Unless the investor (speculator ?) is looking for a very quick gain, the implied initial yield may misrepresent the capital value, and hence the price to be offered.

Chapter 4

Development Appraisal of Land

Appraisal of land to a certain extent is different from appraisal of properties. In the previous chapter, we have discussed that land value is a residual figure. This means we derive the residual amount that is available from the income on land after we have accounted for the various production costs as well as the land user's profit margin. In essence, we consider how much we can earn from the economic activities carried out on land and the expenses we have to incur in carrying out such activities before we come to the measurement of land value.

Under this logic, we can say that land value is derived from property value. Hence, the higher the property prices, the higher the residual sum available and hence the more the developer can afford to pay for land. To some extent, we cannot formulate such an argument as "the increase in property prices is caused by the increase in land price." In fact, it is quite the opposite that is the normal market phenomenon. Land price is high because there is a strong demand in the property market driving up the property prices. Developers having sensed the increase in property prices will bid more for land, which is limited in supply. Developers are able to do so because they know the residual amount available for land is now higher. This in turn sets the new market land price and will become a cost factor of subsequent development projects. Hence, movement in land price is a result of property market fluctuations and not a cause. This is evident when the property market shrinks. Price levels of new projects coming on to the market will fall as well and some times lower than the price level of the secondary market (One of the best examples is the roller-coaster type of residential market in Ma On Shan, New Territories, from 1992 to 1995). This shows that property price levels are more under the influence of market demands (whether speculative or pure investment demands) than under the influence of land price.

APPRAISAL MODEL — RESIDUAL VALUATION

If we accept that land value is a residual value, then market comparison of land price may not be a reliable method in assessing land value. As a result, the residual valuation model has been developed to help solve this problem.

With residual valuation, we start by looking at the income to be generated from land, or the Gross Development Value (GDV in short). The GDV is normally the unit price of property multiplied by the gross floor area, if the property units are to be sold. If the development is meant to be income-producing property, then the investment method can be applied to find the capital value of the development. The GDV represents what we can earn from developing the site. However, in realizing this income we need to spend on certain items as costs. These items need to be deducted from the GDV before we can arrive at the residual figure. The following represents the flow of events:

Gross Development Value:

GDV = Unit price HK$ × Gross Floor Area (GFA) or

GDV = Market rent p.a. divided by market yield × GFA

LESS

1. Construction Costs = Unit cost × GFA
2. Professional Fees eg. Architects, Quantity Surveyors = % × item (1)
3. Marketing and Agency Fees = % × GDV
4. Bank Interest on Costs
5. Contingency = % × (items [1] and [2])
6. Developer's Profit

EQUAL TO

Residual Amount = Land value + Acquisition/
Legal Fees + Bank interest

We can note from the above that after the deduction of the costs and profit items from the GDV figure, we are left with a residual amount that includes not only the land value itself but also acquisition fees and bank interest accrued during the development period. There is therefore a need for a conversion process to further derive the residual land value from this residual amount. This process will be explained in detail in the examples below. First of all, let us discuss the various items in the flow chart above.

The residual valuation model is one of the traditional valuation models developed a long time ago. Similarly to the term and reversion models in the appraisal of real estate, there are certain assumptions to be made in the valuation process. The first one is the assumption that all expenditure and income occur as a single sum at a specific point of time, as if we pay our contractor and architect a lump sum at the beginning of the construction period. This, however, is not the standard practice in the construction industry. Furthermore, we assume all the market information on property prices and rentals will remain the same at the date of completion of the project. Again, this is not realistic. Below, we will give some examples to show the mechanism of the residual valuation model and then an explanation of this model will be follow.

Traditional Residual Valuation Model

Example 6 is the hypothetical land sale data of a piece of land in the Northeastern part of the New Territories. The land is zoned for residential purposes and allows for a gross floor area (GFA) of 120,000 sq.ft. with 65 car parking spaces. In addition, no retail units are allowed. The developer in preparing his maximum bid at the land auction assumes that the current market price for this kind of property in the region is about HK$4150.00 per square foot. In addition, car-parking space is selling at HK$250,000 per unit. This gives him a total development value of this project of HK$514,250,000.00. In other words, he will expect to receive this sum of money on completion of his project when he sells all the property and car parking units.

EXAMPLE 6

NE New Territories

Residential sale price psf			$4,150.00
GFA sq.ft.			120,000.00
GDV Residential			$498,000,000.00
Carpark sale price:			$250,000.00
No. of carpark:			65
Value of carpark:			$16,250,000.00
Total GDV			$514,250,000.00
LESS COSTs and PROFIT			
Building Costs	two years		
$ psf for residential		$600.00	$72,000,000.00
Carpark ($ psf):		$330.00	$2,895,750.00
Total:			$74,895,750.00
Professional Fees		5.00%	$3,744,787.50
Interest on Above		9.00%	$7,396,142.55
Agency+Marketing fees	on GDV	2%	$10,285,000.00
Contingency	on Costs	5%	$3,932,026.88
Development Profit	on GDV	20%	$102,850,000.00
Total Costs + Profit		=	$203,103,706.93
Amount Available for Land; Acquisition and Interest			$311,146,293.07

Let "X" be the Land Value Acquisition cost = 0.03X
Interest on Land for 2 Years = 1.03X times 1.1881   Therefore:
1.223743X = $311,146,293.07

Residual Land Value =	**$254,257,873.65**
Accommodation Value =	**$2,118.82 psf**

However, in order to realize this income, the developer also has to pay some costs. These include the sums owed to the contractors, building professionals, bank interest on costs and marketing fees. The table of Example 6 shows an item called "contingency." This serves as an insurance plan for the un-expected rise of the construction costs (this is why it is based on a percentage of the construction cost). Unexpected increase in the construction can result under different circumstances. One of them is delay in construction caused by bad weather. In Hong Kong, if the construction period overlaps with a typhoon season in the summer, there is a high possibility of having rainy days which may mean delay in the work. This cannot be accounted for accurately by increasing the construction cost unit rate. We therefore insert an additional item to allow for a lump sum figure based on a percentage of the construction costs.

The developer's own remuneration comes from the developer's profit item. In the above example, we put down 20% of GDV as the estimate of a proper return on capital. If it looks too small a figure for property investment to some readers, we can examine the implication of this 20% figure. Since this is a percentage on the GDV, this already includes "profit on profit" from the sale price of the properties units. We can look at this profit figure on the basis of the capital outlay that the developer has to make. In Example 6, the profit figure is HK$102,850,000.00. In the development project, he has to spend a total development capital of HK$411,400,000.00 (i.e. total construction costs and associated expenses of HK$100,253,706.9 [i.e. the total costs and profit figure of HK$203,103,706.93 minus the profit figure of HK$102,850,000] plus land price and all other associated costs in the land transaction). Therefore, profit as a percentage of capital outlay is: $\dfrac{102850000}{411400000} = 25\%$.

We may immediately find from the residual valuation in Example 6 that some aspects are not logical enough to represent the cash flow pattern of a real estate development project. The most obvious one is the fact that payment and receipt of cash do not occur as a lump sum but more often than not through instalments. As a result, if cash inflow and outflow are made equally through a certain number of instalments, the present value of the first instalment will be quite different from the present value of the last instalment especially if the development period is long and inflation during the period is high. In this respect, the model itself has a "self-adjusting" mechanism to offset this error, through the peculiar calculation of the bank interest on cost.

In the traditional residual valuation model, the bank interest payment, although still assumed to be paid out in a lump sum, is calculated through one of the following three ways:

1. $\dfrac{\text{Full Cost}}{2} \times (1 + i\%)^n$ minus $\dfrac{\text{Full Cost}}{2}$

2. Full Cost $\times (1 + i\%/2)^n$ minus Full Cost
3. Full Cost $\times (1 + i\%)^{n/2}$ minus Full Cost

The main objective of these three interest payment calculation methods is to average out the amount of interest payment so as to offset the effect of assuming interest is paid out as a lump sum, which would be greater than the summation of the present value of all the instalment payments of bank interest. The first method (which is adopted in the example) is the assumption that only half of the full cost is being borrowed. The second method is the assumption that only half of the current interest rate is being charged and finally the last method is to assume that only half of the development period carries the burden of bank interest payments.

Such devices, as far as the author is concerned, are only self-deceiving. This is because the divergence in the present values and the book value of other items in the model is also substantial and care should be taken in assessing the actual payments and receipts a developer is getting from a project in present value terms. We will come back to this point in detail, but first let us examine the residual valuation model as a mechanism to assess land value.

The model aims to find the maximum bid that a developer should offer or the minimum bid a land owner should accept. We can work our way through the model topdown. At the very beginning, we have the revenue that a developer can expect from the proceeds of the sale of the project (i.e. HK$514,250,000.00). Then we deduct all the costs including developer's profit incurred during the process of development (i.e. HK$203,703,106). We therefore arrive at a residual sum (i.e. HK$311,146,293). We should be very careful that this residual amount does not represent the land value only but all other associated costs in the process of the land transaction. The importance of this consideration can be seen from this simple calculation:

Assuming that at the completion date we can have HK$200 proceeds from the purchasers of flats and carparks and we need to pay out HK$100 for all the costs and profit. If we assume that the residual amount of HK$100 is land value, then we may go for this amount as our maximum bid for the land today at the land auction. Let us assume further that the development takes two years and that we are able to outbid others for the land at HK$100 today. This HK$100 for land is only the land cost. There are some associated fees such as legal fees etc. that will be incurred immediately after the auction. If such costs amount to 3% of land cost, we shall have to spend HK$103 today. But this is not the end of the story. During the two years of development, there will be bank interest or opportunity costs incurred on the land and other costs (i.e. the HK$103). If the interest rate is 9% p.a., by the time of completion of project, the developer will owe the bank: HK$103 $\times$ (1 + 9%)^2 = HK$122.4. This is obviously larger than the anticipated residual amount of HK$100! When there is a shortage of cash to pay this bill for land costs, the developer will probably have to cut his own profit! We therefore know that the maximum amount for the land should be less than HK$100. In fact, the most ideal situation is that the amount for land value plus all the associated costs plus bank interest should be equal to the exact amount of the residual sum.

Hence, we know that there is a need to single out the land value from the residual amount. Mathematically, we can deduce the land value figure by first assuming it to be value "X." If the associated costs amount to 3% of land value, the total land cost is 1.03X. This is what we did in the above example. Upon completion of the project, the total land cost will be: 1.03X multiplied by 1.1881, the compound interest payment factor. The result 1.223743X should be equal to the residual amount for land, acquisition fees and interest on land: HK$311,146,293. As a result, we divide this residual sum by 1.223743 to arrive at the land value for X which is HK$254,257,873.65.

Now, we can work our way backwards to prove that this is the maximum figure for the value of this land. If we successfully outbid other developers at the auction today and pay HK$254,257,873.65, we shall have to pay a total of HK$261,885,609.8 today (i.e. HK$254,257,873.65 times 1.03). If we take a loan on the HK$261,885,609.8 today, in two years' time, we will owe our banker a total of HK$311,146,293 if we pay an interest rate of 9% p.a. for two years. This amount can be compensated for exactly by the residual amount that we are left with on the completion date of our project, after we have paid out all the necessary costs including a compensation for ourselves.

The above example shows the situation where we sell all our units on completion date. What if we keep part of our development for investment purposes and settle for getting income from the property instead of a one-off purchase price? Example 7 gives another illustration. Here, we have a situation where the conditions of sale of the land allow a certain area in the development to be used for retail purposes. However, the developers interested in this piece of land intend to keep the retail portion under their ownership and rent the units out for a constant income flow in the future.

EXAMPLE 7

North New Territories

Residential sale price psf			$3,600.00
GFA sq.ft.			1,200,000.00
GDV Residential			$4,320,000,000.00
Retail Annual Rental psf @$/sq.ft/mth = HK$100			$1,200.00
GFA sq.ft			68000.00
YP in perp.	All Risk Yield =	8%	$12.50
GDV Retail			$1,020,000,000.00
Car park sale price:			$300,000.00
No. of parking spaces:			100
Value of car parking spaces			$30,000,000.00
Total GDV			$5,370,000,000.00
LESS COSTS and PROFIT			
Building Costs	two years		
$ psf for residential		750	$900,000,000.00
$ psf for retail		550	$37,400,000.00
$ psf for car park		330	$4,455,000.00
Total:			$941,855,000.00
Professional Fees		6.00%	$56,511,300.00
Interest on Above		9.50%	$99,349,926.43
Agency + Marketing fees	on GDV	3%	$161,100,000.00
Contingency	on Costs	5%	$49,918,315.00
Development Profit	on GDV	20%	$1,074,000,000.00
Total Costs + Profit		=	$2,382,734,541.43
Amount Available for Land; Acquisition and Interest			$2,987,265,458.57

Let "X" be the Land Value Acquisition cost = 0.03X

Interest on Land for 2 Years = 1.03X times 1.199025   Therefore:
1.234996X = \$2,987,265,458.57

Residual Land Value =	**\$2,418,846,751.96**
Accommodation Value =	**\$1,907.61 psf**

Basically, the table of Example 7 is the same model as the previous example except that there is a third element in the GDV component, i.e. the retail GDV. The retail GDV is obtained by means of the investment method of valuation. If we still remember the investment method of valuation from the previous chapter, we know that for any income producing properties, the capital value of the property can be obtained by the following formula: Value $= \dfrac{Income}{Yield}$. If the market yield in retail property in this neighbourhood is 8%,[1] and rental income for similar retail properties is about HK\$100 per sq.ft. per month, then the capital value of the retail portion is:

$$\frac{\$1,200}{0.08} \times 68,000 \text{ sq.ft.} = \text{HK}\$1,020,000,000$$

Here we assume that if the retail units are to be sold on the completion date, the value of the properties will be worth the sum of HK\$1,020,000,000.

In Examples 6 and 7, there is a further item at the lowest section of the table called accommodation value (or AV). This is another way of expressing the land value in terms of the gross floor area allowed on the site (i.e. land value divided by GFA). This is a convenient measure of land value based on GFA as we know immediately the proportion of land value as a cost in the overall selling price of the properties. In addition, some times comparison of unit land price based on site area is not as accurate as comparison of unit land price based on GFA. This is true

---

[1] Market yields or all risk yields for different kinds of properties in Hong Kong can be found in the new supplement rental, *Price and Supply Statistics for Major Property Categories*, of the *Property Review* published by the Rating and Valuation Department of Hong Kong.

when two sites have the same GFA allowed but one of them has to provide a substantial amount of open area on the site.

Furthermore, we can observe from above that there are some problems in the traditional residual valuation method that might hinder the use of this model as a valuation tool for the appraisal of land value. The major problem of this model is the inability to account for any fluctuations of cash inflow and outflow during the development. As a result, we will introduce a revised model of this residual valuation method and hope that a more accurate way of assessing land value can be formulated.

Example 8 shows a real case of a land auction in Hong Kong in 1995, for a high class residential development on the Peak. When this site was sold, it became a new indicator of the residential market in that area as supply of land on the Peak has been very scarce. Although the land price estimated from the residual model is very close to the actual market price at the auction, it is pure coincidence, as it turns out, since the site is situated on a slope, resulting in a much higher construction cost than the one assumed in the model below.

EXAMPLE 8

November, 1995 Peak, Mount Kellett Road

Use: Residential			
Residential sale price psf			$13,000.00
GFA sq.ft.			$13,380.00
GDV Residential			$173,940,000.00
Total GDV			$173,940,000.00
LESS COSTS and PROFIT			
Building Costs	two years		
$ psf for residential		1000	$13,380,000.00
Total:			$13,380,000.00
Professional Fees		5.00%	$669,000.00
Interest on Above	(Prime Rate + 2%)	11.00%	$1,630,386.45
Agency + Marketing fees	on GDV	2%	$3,478,800.00
Contingency	on Costs	0%	$0.00
Development Profit	on GDV	20%	$34,788,000.00
Total Costs + Profit		=	$53,946,186.45
Amount Available for Land; Acquisition and Interest			$119,993,813.55

Let "X" be the Land Value Acquisition cost = 0.03X

Interest on Land for 2 Years = 1.03X times	1.2321	
1.269063X	=	$119,993,813.55
Residual Land Value =		**$94,553,078.57**
Accommodation Value =		**$7,066.7 psf**

Similarly, Example 9 also represents a real case of residential land in Taipo sold in 1996 for low rise residential development.

EXAMPLE 9

August, 1996 Taipo Lot TPTL 118			Low Rise Residential
Residential sale price psf			$4,500.00
GFA sq.ft.			228,197.00
GDV Residential			$1,026,886,500.00
Total GDV			$1,026,886,500.00
LESS COSTS and PROFIT			
Building Costs	two years		
$ psf for residential		1000	$228,197,000.00
Total:			$228,197,000.00
Professional Fees		5.00%	$11,409,850.00
Interest on Above	(Prime Rate + 2%)	11.00%	$27,806,374.94
Agency + Marketing fees	on GDV	2%	$20,537,730.00
Contingency	on Costs	15%	$35,941,027.50
Development Profit	on GDV	20%	$205,377,300.00
Total Costs + Profit		=	$529,269,282.44
Amount Available for Land; Acquisition and Interest			$497,617,217.56
Let "X" be the Land Value Acquisition cost = 0.03X			
Interest on Land for 2 Years = 1.03x times 1.2321 = 1.26906X			
1.26906X = $497,617,217.56 Hence:			
Residual Land Value =			**$392,113,880.52**
Accommodation Value =			**$1,718.31 psf**

Example 10 shows the appraisal of a hypothetical site in Central which allows office use. The developer carrying out the appraisal is looking at a short term holding period for the completed development for income purposes and then to resell it when the market price of office premises is more appealing. However, it can be exhibited below that the traditional residual valuation model in development appraisal cannot reflect this special requirement. The model used in appraisal of land value in Example 10 does not distinguish itself in this respect from the previous examples. An alternative model (Example 10a) will be examined for this purpose in a later section.

EXAMPLE 10

Details: Max. GFA: (sq.ft.)   950,000 sq.ft.
          Use of land: Grade A Office in Central
          Open Market Rent psf/month = $75.00
          market yield: 8%

Annual rentals:			$855,000,000.00
GDV			$10,687,500,000.00
Total GDV			$10,687,500,000.00
LESS COSTS and PROFIT			
Building Costs	two years		
$ psf for office		1100	$1,045,000,000.00
Total:			$1,045,000,000.00
Professional Fees		5.00%	$52,250,000.00
Interest on Above		11.00%	$127,335,862.50
Agency + Marketing fees	on GDV	2%	$213,750,000.00
Contingency	on Costs	0%	$0.00
Development Profit	on GDV	25%	$2,671,875,000.00
Total Costs + Profit		=	$4,110,210,862.50
Amount Available for Land; Acquisition and Interest			$6,577,289,137.50

Let "X" be the Land Value Acquisition cost = 0.03X
Interest On Land for 2 Years = 1.03X times   1.2321
1.269063X   = $6,577,289,137.50

Residual Land Value =	**$5,182,791,664.01**
Accommodation Value =	**$5,455.57 psf**

Improved Residual Valuation — D.C.F. model

We have seen in the previous chapter the basic mechanism of the D.C.F. model. In this section, we will take one step further by trying to apply the D.C.F. model to appraisal of land value. The biggest advantage of the D.C.F. model in the development appraisal process is the ability to turn the development into a "digitized picture" of development cash flow so that apart from finding the maximum land value, the developer can have an idea of his financial situation during the development period. Now, based on the above two examples, let us convert the figures from the D.C.F. model for the appraisal of land value.

In this improved model (in Example 6a), we will assume that payment of cash is made in eight equal instalments, i.e. quarterly. In actual fact, there is no limitation that the amount of payment in each instalment has to be equal. It can be alternatively assumed, for example, that 60% of the total cost is paid out in the first month, and the rest is spread evenly over each of the following quarters. Hence, there are eight rows in the model each representing the cash inflow and outflow in each quarter. The first column shows the quarter. The second column is the cash inflow column. We find that most of the rows are empty in the early quarters until quarter seven when we assume that the developer is starting to pre-sell the residential units near the end of the project, but before actual occupation takes place. Cash inflow in the last quarter represents the proceeds from the sale of the car parking spaces at the completion date.

Columns 3 and 4 are the major cost items, i.e. construction costs and professional fees. There is a difference in the cost in quarters 1–4 and the same item in quarters 5–8. This is due to incorporation of the effect of inflation after one year. This cannot be achieved in the traditional residual valuation model.

Column 5 is the interest payments for all the loans from the bank. Such loans include construction costs, professional fees and land cost. In particular, the calculation of interest on land cost is somewhat tricky. This is because land value at this point is still an unknown. In theory, we cannot find the interest on land cost based on the unknown. However, with the advent of the computer, this problem can be solved. In most of the popular computer software especially for calculation, such as Lotus 123 or Microsoft Excel, there is a calculation function that allows for iterated circular-referencing. Hence, we can circular-reference an unknown until this unknown figure is found after repeated trial and error.

Column 6 is the Tax/Agency fees expenses. Again, tax such as stamp duty on land transactions is obtained through the circular-referencing function of the computer programme. Agency fees are incurred when the developer sells his property

Example 6(a)

Approximation of Residual Land Values by D.C.F. Model

Acquisition fees				3%
Use: Residential				
Discount rate	p.a.	=		10.00%
Discount rate	per quarter	=		2.41%
Cost of Capital		=		9.00%
Professional fees:		=		5.00%
Agency + Marketing		=		2.00%
Development period		=	Inflation 10%	2
Construction costs (residential):	600 HK$/sq.ft.		p.a.	
Construction costs (carpark):	330 HK$/sq.ft.			
Sales price (residential) at completion date:	5200 HK$/sq.ft.			
GFA:	120,000.00 sq.ft.			
Sales price (carpark) at completion date:	$300,000.00			
Interest is repaid half-yearly				
Developer's profit:	20.00%			

DISCOUNTED CASH FLOW ANALYSIS FOR LAND PRICE

(1) quarter	(2) CASH INFLOW	(3) CASH OUTFLOW Contr. cost	(4) Fees	(5) interest	(6) Tax + Agency	(7) profit	(8) NET CASH INFLOW	(9) PV FACTOR	(10) Present Value
1	$0	$9,361,969	$468,098		$8,576,337		($18,406,404)	0.976454	($17,973,008)
2	$0	$9,361,969	$468,098	$16,580,271			($26,410,338)	0.953463	($25,181,268)
3	$0	$9,361,969	$468,098				($9,830,067)	0.931012	($9,151,915)
4	$0	$9,361,969	$468,098	$16,580,271			($26,410,338)	0.909091	($24,009,397)
5	$0	$10,298,166	$514,908				($10,813,074)	0.887685	($9,598,609)
6	$0	$10,298,166	$514,908	$16,580,271			($27,393,344)	0.866784	($23,744,116)
7	$624,000,000	$10,298,166	$514,908		12480000		$600,706,926	0.846375	($50,842,325)
8	$19,500,000	$10,298,166	$514,908	$16,580,271		128700000	($136,593,344)	0.826446	($112,887,052)

Residual Land Price = **$285,877,891.7**

Accommodation Value = **$2,382.3**

through property agents. Column 7 records the profit figure which the developer will only realize after he has paid out all other expenses. Hence this cash outflow will only occur in the last quarter.

Finally, net cash inflow is column 2 minus all expense columns (3–7) for each quarter. These net cash inflows (which can be positive or negative) will then be discounted to reflect their present values. In the discounting process, care should be taken in the choice of the discount rate. In this D.C.F. model, it is assumed that the annual discount rate is 10%. As we are dis-counting quarterly cash inflows, a normal practice is to divide this discount rate by 4. A more sensible way however can be achieved as follows:

If: $(1 + I\%) = (1 + i\%)^4$ where I% is the annual rate and i% is the quarterly rate

Then: $\sqrt[4]{(1 + I\%)} = (1 + i\%)$ hence: $i\% = \sqrt[4]{(1 + I\%)} - 1$.

In the example, if our annual rate is 10%, then the ideal quarterly discount rate should be: $\sqrt[4]{(1 + 10\%)} - 1 = 2.41\%$

Once we add all the present values of the net cash inflows from each quarter together, we have the land value at present date value. This is because the net present values of cash inflows for each quarter represent a residual amount in each quarter. The final figure in the D.C.F. model represents the total residual land value.

In addition, we may notice from the D.C.F. model that the selling prices of different property types are quite different from the selling prices used in the residual valuation model. This is because we can state here that the selling prices are the expected selling prices at the completion date, which makes the calculation more sensible than the traditional residual valuation model.

From this example, we can show that provided the forecast-ing job is done properly, we can have a higher AV under the D.C.F. model. In other words, the developer having his analysis done in the D.C.F. model can outbid the developer using the residual valuation model since the former developer is analysing the market in the future where cash flows actually vary. In addition, this successful developer has incorporated as many variations as he can expect in the development process such that he has turned the whole physical development into a spreadsheet in financial terms.

Nevertheless, it is the very advantage of the D.C.F. model that betrays the model itself. A major condition for a reliable D.C.F. model is the accurate reflection of future values such as selling prices and construction costs. In the property market, few experts can claim to be able to predict this aspect. Despite this drawback, the author still thinks it is a much better appraisal model than the traditional residual valuation model because of the flexibility it allows. The example below shows the application of the D.C.F. model for the appraisal of land when part of the development is used for investment purposes and not for sale. In the following section, a discussion will be made on the application of the D.C.F. model not for the appraisal of land value but for the appraisal of the development project itself. But first of all we can examine the effect of apply D.C.F. to the development appraisal of land value based on data from the traditional residual valuation examples above. The following shows a simple analysis of the residual land values (in the format of accommodation value) based on the two models and their assumptions:

Example	Traditional Residual Model	Example	D.C.F. Model
7	$1,908/sq.ft.	7a	$1,821/sq.ft.
8	$7,067/sq.ft.	8a	$7,971/sq.ft.
9	$1,718/sq.ft.	9a	$2,067/sq.ft.
10	$5,456/sq.ft.	10a	$4,966/sq.ft.

The discrepancies in the two models reflect the way that the assumptions as well as the interrelationship among the assumptions adopted in the two models determine to a large extent the residual land value. In the traditional residual model, all data is market current data as no forecasting is usually made. In addition, all payments, such as construction costs, professional fees and interest payments are made at a single point of time whereas in the D.C.F. model such payments are made at various points during the development period and discounted to reflect the present values.

Example 7(a)

Approximation of Residual Land Values by D.C.F. model

Acquisition fees | | 3%

Use: Residential

Discount rate	per annum	=	10.00%
Discount rate	per quarter	=	2.41%
Cost of Capital		=	9.50%
Professional fees:		=	6.00%
Agency + Marketing		=	3.00%
Development period		=	2

residential

Construction costs: | 750 HK$/sq.ft.
Sales price at completion date: | 3850 HK$/sq.ft.

GFA: | 120,000.00 sq.ft.

retail

Construction costs: | 550 HK$/sq.ft.
rent at completion date: | 1320 HK$/sq.ft./year

GFA:	68000	All risk yield	=			8.0%

Car Parking spaces

Construction costs: $330.00 HK$/sq.ft.

price at completion date: $350,000.00

area per space (sq.ft.): 135   No. of car park: 100

Interest is repaid half-yearly   Inflation = 10% p.a.

Developer's profit: 20.00%

DISCOUNTED CASH FLOW ANALYSIS FOR LAND PRICE

quarter	CASH INFLOW	CASH OUTFLOW Contr. cost	Fees	interest	Tax + Agency	profit	NET INCOME	PV FACTOR	Present Value
1	$0	$117,731,875	$7,063,913				($194,092,829)	0.976454	($189,522,734)
2	$0	$117,731,875	$7,063,913	$159,513,835			($284,309,622)	0.953463	($271,078,583)
3	$0	$117,731,875	$7,063,913				($124,795,788)	0.931012	($116,186,427)
4	$0	$117,731,875	$7,063,913	$159,513,835			($284,309,622)	0.909091	($258,463,282)
5	$0	$129,505,063	$7,770,304				($137,275,366)	0.887685	($121,857,351)
6	$4,620,000,000	$129,505,063	$7,770,304	$159,513,835	138600000		$4,184,610,799	0.866784	$3,627,154,175
7	$0	$129,505,063	$7,770,304				($137,275,366)	0.846375	($116,186,423)
8	$1,157,000,000	$129,505,063	$7,770,304	$159,513,835	0	1155400000	($295,189,201)	0.826446	($243,957,997)

| | | | | | $69,297,041 | | | | |

Residual Land Price = $2,309,901,378.58

Accommodation Value = **$1,821.69**

Example 8(a)

Approximation of Residual Land Values by D.C.F. model
Site: November, 1995 Peak, Mount Kellett Road

Acquisition fees			3%
Use: Residential			
Discount rate	p.a.	=	10.00%
Discount rate	per quarter	=	2.41%
Cost of Capital		=	11.00%
Professional fees:		=	5.00%
Agency + Marketing		=	2.00%
Development period		=	2
Construction costs:		$1,000.00 HK$/sq.ft.	
Sales price at completion date:		$16,032.09 HK$/sq.ft.	(assuming a 15% increase in price p.a. for 1.5 years)
GFA:	13,380.00 sq.ft.		
Interest is repaid half-yearly			
Developer's profit:	20.00%		

DISCOUNTED CASH FLOW ANALYSIS FOR LAND PRICE

quarter	CASH INFLOW	CASH OUTFLOW Contr. cost	Fees	interest	Tax + Agency	profit	NET INCOME	PV FACTOR	Present Value
1	$0	$1,672,500	$83,625		$3,199,521		($4,955,646)	0.976454	($4,838,961)
2	$0	$1,672,500	$83,625	$6,677,119			($8,433,244)	0.953463	($8,040,783)
3	$0	$1,672,500	$83,625				($1,756,125)	0.931012	($1,634,974)
4	$0	$1,672,500	$83,625	$6,677,119			($8,433,244)	0.909091	($7,666,585)
5	$0	$1,839,750	$91,988				($1,931,738)	0.887685	($1,714,775)
6	$214,509,350	$1,839,750	$91,988	$6,677,119	42901869.94		$201,610,306	0.866784	$174,752,611
7	$0	$1,839,750	$91,988				($1,931,738)	0.846375	($1,634,974)
8	$0	$1,839,750	$91,988	$6,677,119		42901869.94	($51,510,726)	0.826446	($42,570,845)

Residual Land Price = $106,650,714.01

Accommodation Value = $7,971

Example 9(a)

Approximation of Residual Land Values by D.C.F. model
Site: November, 1996 Taipo Lot TPTL 118

Acquisition fees   3%

Use: Low Rise Residential

Discount rate   p.a.   =   12.00%
Discount rate   per quarter   =   2.87%
Cost of Capital   =   11.00%
Professional fees: =   5.00%
Agency + Marketing   =   2.00%
Development period   =   2

Construction costs: $1,000.00 HK$/sq.ft.
Sales price at completion date: $5,549.57 HK$/sq.ft.   (assuming a 15% increase in price p.a. for 1.5 years)
GFA: 228,197.00 sq.ft.

Interest is repaid half-yearly
Developer's profit: 20.00%

DISCOUNTED CASH FLOW ANALYSIS FOR LAND PRICE

quarter	CASH INFLOW	CASH OUTFLOW Contr. cost	Fees	interest	Tax + Agency	profit	NET INCOME	PV FACTOR	Present Value
1	$0	$28,524,625	$1,426,231		$14,150,031		($44,100,887)	0.972065	($42,868,948)
2	$0	$28,524,625	$1,426,231	$39,779,019			($69,729,876)	0.944911	($65,888,539)
3	$0	$28,524,625	$1,426,231				($29,950,856)	0.918515	($27,510,325)
4	$0	$28,524,625	$1,426,231	$39,779,019			($69,729,876)	0.892857	($62,258,818)
5	$0	$31,377,088	$1,568,854				($32,945,942)	0.867916	($28,594,295)
6	$1,266,395,052	$31,377,088	$1,568,854	$39,779,019	25327901.04		$1,168,342,190	0.843671	$985,696,071
7	$0	$31,377,088	$1,568,854				($32,945,942)	0.820103	($27,019,069)
8	$0	$31,377,088	$1,568,854	$39,779,019		253279010.4	($326,003,972)	0.797194	($259,888,370)

Residual Land Price = $471,667,706.29

Accommodation Value = $2,066.93

In Example 10 above, we have shown that the traditional residual valuation model may not be able to incorporate developer's investment decisions into the development appraisal. In the following example, the basic information from Example 10 is adopted, with the further information that the developer is not very optimistic about the office market upon completion of the project. In addition, the developer would like to retain the development for a short period of five years for constant income flow for the group.

From Example 10a, we can see that to estimate the development value of the completed project, we can estimate the discounted values of the rental incomes that will be generated during the five-year holding period. This is shown in the small table at the bottom of Example 10a. As we assume that market rent will grow by 6% per annum and market capitalization rate is 8%, then the required rate of return to compensate the opportunity cost will be equal to 14%. Accordingly, the developer will discount his future incomes from his 5-year holding period at this rate. After this holding period, the developer will sell the development, at the beginning of year 6. To estimate the re-sale value of the development, we can apply the capitalization method in Example 6a. Hence, we can estimate the rental value at the point of re-sell, i.e. open market rent at the beginning of year 6. Then we will capitalize it at 8%, the market yield which is assumed to be constant all the time. This makes the re-sell value of the project at the beginning of year 6 at: $1,285,603,871.44/8% = HK$16,070,048,393

However, this only represents the capital value at the end of year 5. This figure then needs to be discounted to the date of completion of the project to reflect the GDV basis. As the resell occurs at the beginning of year 6, there is only a need for 5 years' discounting. Hence, the discounting factor is the same as that applied in the year 5's income. Thus, $16,070,048,393 times 0.51936866 equal to $8,346,279,570.05. When this sum is added to the total present value of the 5 years' income during the holding period, this becomes the gross development value of the project at the time of completion, i.e. around $12,008.5 million.

Example 10(a)

Approximation of Residual Land Values by D.C.F. model

Acquisition fees				3%
Use: Office-Grade A				
Discount rate	p.a.	=	14.00%	
Discount rate	per quarter	=	3.29%	
Cost of Capital		=	11.00%	
Professional fees:		=	5.00%	
Agency + Marketing		=	2.00%	
Development period		=	2	
Construction costs:	$1,100.00 HK$/sq.ft.			
OMR-current:	$900.00	increment p.a.:: 6.00%	OMR — 2 years later:	$1,011.24
GFA:	950,000.00 sq.ft.			
Interest is repaid half-yearly				
Developer's profit:	25.00%			

Example 10(a) (Cont'd)

DISCOUNTED CASH FLOW ANALYSIS FOR LAND PRICE

quarter	CASH INFLOW	CASH OUTFLOW Contr. cost	Fees	interest	Tax + Agency	profit	NET INCOME	PV FACTOR	Present Value
1		$0	$130,625,000	$6,531,250		$141,530,370	($278,686,620)	0.968148	($269,809,876)
2		$0	$130,625,000	$6,531,250	$322,838,533		($459,994,783)	0.93731	($431,157,904)
3		$0	$130,625,000	$6,531,250			($137,156,250)	0.907455	($124,463,145)
4		$0	$130,625,000	$6,531,250	$322,838,533		($459,994,783)	0.878551	($404,128,796)
5		$0	$143,687,500	$7,184,375			($150,871,875)	0.850567	($128,326,663)
6		$0	$143,687,500	$7,184,375	$322,838,533		($473,710,408)	0.823475	($390,088,603)
7		$0	$143,687,500	$7,184,375			($150,871,875)	0.797245	($120,281,918)
8	$12,008,475,000	$143,687,500	$7,184,375	$322,838,533		$3,002,118,750.00	$8,532,645,842	0.771852	$6,585,935,918

Residual Land Price = $4,717,679,013.87

Accommodation Value = $4,965.98

Estimation of GDV at end of quarter 8
assuming income reviewed yearly
Investment period:

Year	Rental Income	PV Factor @14%	discounted income
1	$960,678,000.00	0.877192982	$842,700,000.00
2	$1,018,318,680.00	0.769467528	$783,563,157.89
3	$1,079,417,800.80	0.674971516	$728,576,269.62
4	$1,144,182,868.85	0.592080277	$677,448,110.35
5	$1,212,833,840.98	0.519368664	$629,907,892.08
6	$1,285,603,871.44	(1/0.08 × 0.51936)	$8,346,279,570.05
			$12,008,475,000.00

Development Appraisal

In a development project, the first task is to find a good site. Assuming the developer is trying to buy a piece of land either from the government in a land auction or from a private land owner, he is also facing competition. In formulating his bidding strategy, therefore there is a need for the developer to make sure that the bid he is placing is the maximum he can afford. In this respect, a D.C.F. model can show him the alternatives he can have in varying the development process so that he can have a different cash flow programme and hence a different residual land value.

Example 11 in the following is based on the Example 6(a) and it is assumed that all properties will only be sold at the completion date. Hence cash inflow will only occur at that quarter. From this analysis, we know that if the developer is to sell all his units at the completion date, he will be able to afford an AV of HK$2,295 per sq.ft as his maximum bid. However, if somehow he manages to rearrange his selling programme so that he can now offer pre-sell of his properties six months earlier at the same price level, then he can afford a higher AV of HK$2470 per sq.ft. Now he knows that without sacrificing his own profit or other cost elements, he can outbid his competitors up to the new AV level. The same analysis can be applied to other elements in the cash flow programme so that the developer can manoeuvre his development pattern so as to realize the biggest residual value for his bid for the land.

Furthermore, we can also apply the D.C.F. model to sensitivity analysis. Sensitivity analysis is the examination of the variables in the development which will affect the profit figure substantially. We are concerned with the profit here because once the land conversion process has started, the land price figure becomes a cost item and remains as a fixed item. In this case, the residual sum now becomes the developer's profit since this is the only sum to be realized at the end of the development process.

We use Example 6(a) to show the mechanism of sensitivity analysis. Basically, we vary each major variable (which we think will affect the residual profit to a certain extent), one at a time,

Example 11

Approximation of Residual Land Values by D.C.F. model

Acquisition fees			3%
Use: Residential			
Discount rate	p.a.	=	10.00%
Discount rate	per quarter	=	2.41%
Cost of Capital		=	9.00%
Professional fees:		=	5.00%
Agency + Marketing		=	2.00%
Development period		=	2
Construction costs (residential):	600 HK\$/sq.ft.		Inflation 10% p.a.
Construction costs (carpark):	330 HK\$/sq.ft.		
Sales price (residential) at date of pre-sale:	5200 HK\$/sq.ft.		

GFA: 120,000.00 sq.ft.

Sales price (carpark) at completion date: $300,000.00

Interest is repaid half-yearly

Developer's profit: 20.00%

DISCOUNTED CASH FLOW ANALYSIS FOR LAND PRICE

quarter	CASH INFLOW	CASH OUTFLOW Contr. cost	Fees	interest	Tax + Agency	profit	NET INCOME	PV FACTOR	Present Value
1	$0	$9,361,969	$468,098		$8,891,159		($18,721,226)	0.976454	($18,280,418)
2	$0	$9,361,969	$468,098	$17,052,504			($26,882,571)	0.953463	($25,631,526)
3	$0	$9,361,969	$468,098				($9,830,067)	0.931012	($9,151,915)
4	$0	$9,361,969	$468,098	$17,052,504			($26,882,571)	0.909091	($24,438,700)
5	$0	$10,298,166	$514,908				($10,813,074)	0.887685	($9,598,609)
6	$624,000,000	$10,298,166	$514,908	$17,052,504	12480000		($583,654,422)	0.866784	($505,902,382)
7	$0	$10,298,166	$514,908				$10,813,074	0.846375	($9,151,914)
8	$19,500,000	$10,298,166	$514,908	$17,052,504		128700000	($137,065,578)	0.826446	($113,277,328)

Residual Land Price = **$296,371,973.58**

Accommodation Value = **$2,469.77**

while keeping other variables constant. Each time, a new residual profit will be obtained. We record the change of this new profit figure from the original figure. Eventually, we will have a table listing the effect of each variable on profit. For instance, if we increase the bank interest rate by 10% while keeping other variables constant, we notice that profit will drop by 5% only. Hence, the developer's profit is not particularly sensitive to the changes in bank interest rates in this example. On the other hand, if we increase the selling price by 10%, we bring an increase of profit of 45%, or almost 4.5 times the effect of the change in this variable!

The purpose of conducting such a sensitivity analysis is to single out those variables that will contribute to the fluctuation of the residual profit figure. The developer, having identified these variables, can devise some measures to stabilize them so as to stabilize the final profit figure. For instance, if it is found that sale price controls the final profit figure to a great extent, the developer should try to pre-sell his properties as early as possible at the expected price level whereas if construction costs contribute to the fluctuation of profit most, tighter control in the site management should be imposed so as to prevent delay in construction.

As a result, we see that the benefits of application of the D.C.F. model can be manifold due to the fact that the model itself is not just a valuation model, but more an appraisal model. The difference lies on the important fact that while we are valuing the real estate, a simultaneous analysis should also be carried out. In this respect, we are not only giving raw market data, but also a piece of useful analysis for further action by the investor/developer. This is what "professionalism" is meant to be.

From the sensitivity analysis example above, we can observe that the estimation of property prices is most instrumental in the determination of the profitability of the project. In order to produce a relatively reliable result of the gross development value figure, one would need to apply a forecasting model in the examination of the factors affecting property prices. One of these models is the hedonic pricing model. In the following simple example, this regression model is applied in the examination of factors affecting the prices of the two major residential developments in Hong Kong, namely the Laguna City on

Example 12

Sensitivity Analysis for Development Profit:

quarter	CASH INFLOW	CASH OUTFLOW Construction cost	Fees	Interest	Tax +Agency	Land Price	NET INCOME	PV FACTOR	Present Value
1	$0	$9,361,969	$468,098		$8,260,797	275359892	($293,450,756)	0.976454	($286,541,188)
2	$0	$9,361,969	$468,098	$16,106,961			($25,937,028)	0.953463	($24,729,985)
3	$0	$9,361,969	$468,098				($9,830,067)	0.931012	($9,151,915)
4	$0	$9,361,969	$468,098	$16,106,961			($25,937,028)	0.909091	($23,579,115)
5	$0	$10,298,166	$514,908				($10,813,074)	0.887685	($9,598,609)
6	$0	$10,298,166	$514,908	$16,106,961			($26,920,034)	0.866784	($23,333,858)
7	$0	$10,298,166	$514,908				($10,813,074)	0.846375	($9,151,914)
8	$643,500,000	$10,298,166	$514,908	$16,106,961	12870000		$603,709,966	0.826446	$498,933,813
					Profit:				$112,847,229.53

	Increase		Decrease	
Interest Rate	10%	20%	20%	30%
Discount Rate	-5%	-10%	10%	15%
Sale Price (Res.)	-7%	-13%	13%	20%
Costs	45%	90%	-90%	-134%
Inflation	-7%	-15%	15%	22%
	0%	-1%	1%	1%

Kowloon side and the South Horizons development on Hong Kong Island.

Hedonic Pricing Model — Methodology

Hedonic pricing technique, a systematic regression analysis, will be utilized for the assessment of the relationships between the unit price (sale price per square feet) and the various independent variables. This is accomplished by the construction of two separate analyses for the two comprehensive developments.

The two analyses will be based on the same approach and same statistical model form but using different variables. The dependent variable will be the unit price of residential property and the selection criteria for the independent variables will be based on the ideas brought from previous studies and the present situation of the Hong Kong market. Data will then be arranged, sampled, and sifted. As with the model construction, there will be two sets of data for the corresponding developments. The two sets of data will be assigned for two sampling ratios according to the total amount of data available. They are then sifted, and data which is incomplete, or which has different interests attached will be removed. Afterwards, they will be computed through a computer programme in order to select the model form.

The Data

The transactions of domestic premises registered in the Land Office from 15 November, 1994 to 15 November, 1995 as well as the building information available will be utilized as data input for the test model in this study. They are retrieved from the comprehensive records of the Economic Property Research Centre (EPRC) and the Buildings Department respectively.

The EPRC and the Buildings Department provides information of two types. They are firstly the transaction information and secondly the physical characteristics of the transaction units when possible. The transaction information includes the transaction price, the address, the date of transaction and the names of the assignee. Physical characteristics include the date of occupation permit grant, the gross floor area, the usable floor area and the number of stories of a building.

Map analysis and field work have also been carried out. The orientation of the unit and other particular characteristics such as the distance to the nearest transportation mode are obtained from this analysis. The scope of data is first restricted to the period from 15 November, 1994 to 15 November, 1995. This will be called "the period under investigation" hereafter. The aim of this is to reduce the growth and time effect. It is crucial to the analysis results because the longer the period under investigation, the higher the possibility that speculation occurs. Speculation activities cause the purchasers to be less rational in making market decisions.

This approach of restricting the period of transaction has not been attempted in the past by any author, since the amount of data available is very limited. It is, however, possible in this study with the presence of the EPRC system which has substantial price transaction data in this period.

The reason for choosing the so-called "period under investigation" time range is that it is recent and it can reflect a more updated reference to purchasers. Moreover, the government policy[2] of suppressing the residential property price has come into effect which has in turn eliminated the effect of speculation by investors. It is expected that the variation of price will be due to the purchasers' preference which is the main focus of the study.

The areas selected to be the sample clusters are i) Laguna City, Lam Tin, Eastern Kowloon and ii) South Horizons, Ap Lei Chau, Hong Kong Island. The choice of these areas is due to the availability of data from them within the period under investigation. Besides, this type of comprehensive development has similar characteristics, such as design layout, orientation, accessibility, location, amenity facilities, entertainment facilities and they were developed by the same company group, so they are ideal to be used as a controlled comparison.

---

[2] See Chapter Three, General Market.

Transactions on premises from 60 m² to 110 m² square metre in area will be tested under the models. This size range is chosen because this range is the class of transactions average during the period under study.

Sampling of data

Owing to the substantial amount of data from the EPRC database, there are a total of 1113 and 2480 transactions recorded for South Horizons and Laguna City respectively within the defined period of study. Before sampling data, transaction records which indicate other attached interests, such as car park space and roof floor area, were sifted out. They are treated as special cases which need special techniques and judgements when being valued. This ensures a balanced result. The number of transaction records sifted out is 15 in Laguna City and none at all in South Horizons.

In order to make the statistical result fair and non-biased, it is necessary that the size of the data sample should be similar for the two estates. Therefore, the sampling ratio is adjusted to 1:4 for Laguna City and 1:8 for the South Horizon. The method of sampling data is chosen to be as simple as possible. The original transaction records are sorted chronologically, that is, they are arranged in a time series according to the date of the transaction. The records were selected sequentially by spacing with the specified ratio. For example, in the set of transactions in Laguna City with a sampling ratio of 1:4, the first record is selected, then the fifth one, the ninth one and so on. Eventually, the number of samples put into the statistical model is 310 for South Horizon and 275 for Laguna City.

Statistical Tests

The techniques to achieve the above task require the application of computer programmes such as SPSS.[3]

---

[3] SPSS for Windows, Release 6.0 (17 June 1993), Copyright © SPSS Inc., 1989–1993.

t-test

A t-test is a test statistic which shows the significance relationship. After achieving the t-values of each independent variable and the degree of freedom[4] given by the computer printout, the table of t-Distribution is consulted. This table determines the probability (denoted by α) that the null hypothesis (where the estimated coefficient of the independent variable being tested is zero) is rejected.

The relationship between the dependent variable and the independent variable is significant at $(1 - \alpha) \times 100\%$ confidence level if $|t| \geq T_{\alpha,df}$, where $T_{\alpha,df}$ if the tabulated value in t-table corresponds to α, and the degree of freedom is df. The level of confidence can be concluded by checking the tables. Moreover, the advanced feature in the SPSS also shows the level of confidence by checking within its own database. There is a column called "sign T" in the SPSS results showing the level of confidence in an modified format. For instance, if the value of an independent variable is 0.001, this means that the probability of the coefficient of this variable being zero is no more than 0.1%. In other words, this coefficient is significantly different from zero at 98% level of confidence.

In this study, an independent variable will classify as irrelevant to the dependent variable if its level of significance is less than 90%. A variable will be excluded from the model when it is found to be insignificant with the unit price.

Correlation analysis

The problem of "multicollinearity" often exists among dependent variables. Two independent variables included in the model will contribute redundant information since they have been correlated with each other. In this study, an independent variable is considered to be highly collinear with other variables if the correlation coefficient of them is greater than 0.7.[5] In case that there is collinearity, one of the variables must be excluded.

---

[4] The degree of freedom in a model is the sample size less the number of dependent and independent variables.

[5] 0.7 is a subjective value determined by the author, there is no clear cut answer to how great of the correlation contribute problem to the model.

R^2 (Residual sum of square)

The residual sum of square, R^2, represents the fitness of a functional form to the data. It is used to measure the extent of movement in the dependent variable that is explained by the independent variables in a function. The value of R^2, ranging from 0 to 1, which indicates complete lack of fit to perfect fit respectively, will also be reported in the SPSS results.

In this study, the model consists of more than one independent variable. It is a multi-variables equation. Therefore, the measure of fitness is changed to an adjusted residual sum of the square. The adjusted R^2 is similar to R^2 but it is used in the multi-variables model.

Development of the Model

After making reference to the previous studies, eight determinants are selected. These determinants are transformed into ten independent variables which fit the format of the statistical model.

Model Form 1 (Linear)
$$Y = \beta_0 + \beta_1 X_1 + \beta_2 X_2 + \ldots + \beta_n X_n$$

Model Form 2 (Logarithm)
$$Y = \beta_0 + \beta_1 \log X_1 + \beta_2 \log X_2 + \ldots + \beta_n \log X_n$$

Model Form 3 (Log-linear)
$$\log Y = \beta_0 + \beta_1 \log X_1 + \beta_2 \log X_2 + \ldots + \beta_n \log X_n$$

Model Form 4 (Semi-log)
$$\log Y = \beta_0 + \beta_1 X_1 + \beta_2 X_2 + \ldots + \beta_n X_n$$

Firstly, different functional forms are used on a trial basis with the same set of parameters. Afterwards, one of them will be selected. The selection criterion for the final form will depend on the comparison among the adjusted residual sum of square (R^2). If R^2 is a high value, it means that the selected variables computed in the model explain more of the variations caused. Since the dependent variables of Model Form 3 and Model Form

4 are different to the other two, the original dependent variable, Y, will be replaced by Y^{*6} on the equation for comparison in order to obtain a meaningful comparison of residual sum of square.

The dependent variable of this model is defined as the unit price of the transacted premises. The detailed calculation of this important variable will be shown in the following section.

The set of independent variables selected is categorized into three groups. One of the groups is the physical character of the premises which includes i) age; ii) gross floor area of the units; iii) the loss ratio, iv) the number of storeys in the building; v) the vertical ratio and vi) the orientation. The second group is the location variables, they include i) the walking distance to the transport node or terminus and ii) the walking distance to the nearest shopping arcade. Finally, there is the time variable on a monthly basis. The time factor is being considered, even though the data comes from transactions within a year period, because there may be growth in the capital value during the period which is unavoidable.

Variable	Variable Description	Data Source
PRICE	The transaction unit price of the unit registered in Land Office.	Data Base in Economic Property Research Centre (EPRC)
AGE	Age of the Building in term of month.	Occupation permit in monthly statistics published by Building Department.
GROSS	Gross Floor Area of the transacted unit.	Calculation from EPRC
LOSS	Loss Factor, this is the ratio of non-usable floor area to gross floor area of the unit.	Calculation from EPRC

---

[6] $Y^* = c * Y$, where $c = \exp\{-(\Sigma \log Y)/(n)\}$, i.e. the inverse of the geometric mean of Y.

(Cont'd)

Variable	Variable Description	Data Source
VERT	Vertical location of the unit.	Calculation from EPRC and Occupation Permit.
DISTT	Walking distance between the building entrance and the nearest transportation node/terminus.	Map Analysis and field work.
DISTS	Walking distance between the building entrance and the nearest shopping arcade.	Map Analysis and field work.
(ORIN)	Orientation of the unit with reference to the east orientation.	Map Analysis and field work.
(ORIS)	Same as above.	Map Analysis and field work.
(ORIW)	Same as above.	Map Analysis and field work.
TIME	The transaction period of the unit. This is measured monthly where the entry of "1" means November, 1994, and so on.	Occupation permit in monthly statistics published by Building Department.

Results for the Selection of Model Form

The SPSS results, by comparing the adjusted residual sum of square of each form, show that the linear form has the highest value among all models. No matter which set of data is being put into the programme, it is found that linear forms seems to have the best result. Therefore, this form is chosen as the model for further tests.

The choice of linear form may imply that there is a simple linear relation between the unit price of residential flats and the scope of variables chosen. The linear relationship has reached a satisfactory level. It should be understood that a simple model is preferable to a complex one provided that their power of explanation is similar. This is because modelling should be a simple way which people are looking for to explain some phenomenon.

An Analysis of Results for South Horizons

Table 4 Regression Results (South Horizons)

Independent Variable	Coefficient	t-value		Beta-coefficient
AGE	−4.7396	−2.360	***	−0.2709
DISTS	−1.2461	−4.406	***	−0.0484
GROSS	0.8841	5.920	***	0.0539
LOSS	−53.7060	−117.508	***	−1.0041
ORIN	−152.0569	−3.427	***	−0.0293
TIME	−34.9064	−4.600	***	−0.0938
VERT	370.2377	5.496	***	0.0449
(Constant)	5283.6665	35.322	***	

Functional Form: Linear
Dependent Variable: PRICE
Degree of Freedom: 302
Adjusted R^2: 0.97980

*** Coefficient is significantly different from zero at 98% level of confidence.

The regression results for the model of South Horizons show an adjusted residual sum of square of the model value at 0.98026. Seven variables remain in the model. Three variables have been excluded from the model. None of them has been excluded for the reason of high correlation. The SPSS programmes show that the excluded variables have little influence on the unit price in the South Horizons analysis. The excluded variables are DISTT, ORIS and ORIW.

Excluded variables

DISTT is excluded from the model because it has little influence on the unit price in the South Horizons analysis. The justification is that buses departing from the bus terminal have to pass through the South Horizons Drive before leaving South Horizons. Since the South Horizons Drive is a road passing through the whole estate and there are three bus stops all around, passengers are able to board almost anywhere within the estate. This explains the phenomenon that purchasers have little concern for where the bus terminal is.

The other excluded variables are the dummy variables, ORIS and ORIW, representing the orientation of south and west respectively. The justification of their exclusion will be discussed later in the paragraph concerning the physical character variables.

Location variables

DISTS is not excluded from the model, on the contrary, it is found to be highly significant with the unit prices. The negative sign for the coefficient of DISTS is shown as originally expected. The result implies that the unit price of the building will be declined about HK$1.25 if it is one metre further away from the nearest shopping arcade. The result is very reasonable as a convenient arcade is vital for a very isolated estate such as South Horizons.

However, to the variable DISTT, which should theoretically have the same importance as DISTS does, is excluded in the model. The justification mentioned in the previous section makes the situation different. It is believed that it would have a similar significant effect if there was only one bus stop, even if it sounds less plausible.

Physical variables

Generally speaking, AGE, GROSS, LOSS and VERT perform well in the South Horizons model, as expected. They are found to be highly significant to the unit price in the model. Regarding the SPSS results, the variable, AGE, achieve an absolute t-value of 2.360 and an coefficient of –4.396. This implies that the unit price will drop HK$4.74 per square foot if the transacted property is one month older. That means that the instantaneous annual decline rate is HK$56.88 per square foot, about 1.26% of the mean unit price. Even though this seems a small figure compared with unit price, it is statistically significant in the model. Moreover, we should remember that real estate property could typically have a physical life of 60 years or even more. This decline rate might be useful for the property manager in calculating the salvage value of a property.

The variable GROSS bears a positive coefficient with a value of about 0.88. This implies that the unit price should rise HK$0.88 as the gross area increases by one square foot. If the gross area of the premises increases from 638 square feet to 1100 square feet, the unit price will have an increment of HK$407. In fact, this increment is relatively small in magnitude. It is, however, worth remembering that it is significant in the determination of the unit price.

The results show an interesting figure for the variable LOSS, about –53.71. A negative value is obtained as expected because rational purchasers certainly prefer a higher ratio of area where they have exclusive rights. The interesting point is that the regression result implies there will be a drop of HK$53.71 in unit price if the LOSS ratio is increased by 0.01 (1 percentage unit). This drop rate is very close to 1% of the constant of the unit price[7] in the model results.

For instance, the unit price is $5,283.00[8] per square foot if the loss ratio is zero; the unit price will be $2,597.50 per square foot (approximately half of the constant coefficient) if the loss ratio is 50%; and the unit price will drop to zero if the loss ratio is close to 98%.

This result proves the rationality of the purchasers' behaviour. Purchasers will only consider the real exclusive interest they can enjoy when they are thinking about the unit price.

The empirical results of the variable VERT the unit price will be raised by HK$370.24 if the subject property is taken from the first floor to the top floor. Since the total number of storeys for buildings in South Horizons ranges from 30 to 42, it is calculated that the mean is about 33.58 for the data input. Assuming the function is perfectly linear and the difference is the same, the increment will be approximately HK$11.00 for each rise of storey. Of course, the calculation unit should be in vertical ratio if precision is required.

Regardless of the significance of the three orientation dummy variables, it is interesting to discover that the coefficients are opposite in sign to expectations. Remembering that the east

---

[7] Since (Constant)= 5283.67, then 1% x (Constant) = 52.84
[8] Assume normal price equal to the constant coefficient.

orientation is defined to be the reference direction to all orientation dummy variables, it was originally expected that south orientation would have a positive effect on the unit price. However, the regression results show that south orientation made little difference when compared with east or west. On the other hand, north orientation did make the difference. The regression result shows that units with a north orientation are cheaper in unit price compared with an east orientation. The view from the unit accounts for this phenomenon.

From the location map of South Horizons in the Ap Lei Chau Peninsula, it is found that South Horizons is located at on the south-west coast of the peninsula. As a result, it is understood that most of the units facing north have no sea-view from anywhere within the flat. In addition, Aberdeen pier, residential crowds and the Tin Wan manufacturing and factory area, which cause pollution and nuisance, are located exactly to the north of South Horizons. These nuisances are particularly critical for Block 1 to Block 11. In the case of Block 13A to Block 20, the contrast is even stronger, because transport and the shopping arcade are situated due north of them.

The diamond shape layout of South Horizons has the advantage that each unit could have at least two frontages with views. This layout design explains the small difference in unit price among the units with east, south or west prospects.

Time variable

The coefficient value of the time variable, TIME, is −34.91. It has a high absolute t-value of 4.6 showing its significance. The negative sign in front of this coefficient confirms that there was a downward adjustment in the capital values at South Horizons from 15 November, 1994 to 15 November 1995. The unit price declined by HK$34.91 every month.

The results reflect the real situation of the residential property market during that period. After government measures were executed, both the price and the transaction volume of the residential property market was cooled down.

An Analysis of Results for Laguna City

Table 5 Regression Results (Laguna City)

Independent Variable	Coefficient	t-value		Beta-coefficient
AGE	−14.4601	−9.928	***	−0.4493
GROSS	0.5370	−8.381	***	−0.3569
TIME	−59.8742	−5.394	***	−0.2455
VERT	500.1769	4.508	***	0.1914
(Constant)	5733.9179	48.740	***	

Functional Form: Linear
Dependent Variable: PRICE
Degree of Freedom: 270
Adjusted R^2: 0.51360

*** Coefficient is significantly different from zero at 98% level of confidence.

After the stepwise screening input selection, only four variables remain in the model and show significant influence on the unit price, the other six variables being excluded from the model.

The regression results of the Laguna City model are different from those of South Horizons. The most interesting difference is the exclusion of some of the variables. Although there are more variables being excluded from the model for Laguna City, the adjusted residual sum of square still has a value of 0.5136 implying that the functional form can still represent over half of the variance caused by the remaining four. Notwithstanding that both Laguna City and South Horizons are comprehensive development by the same organization bearing many similarities, the behaviour of the predictor variables is not the same.

Since the variables which remained in the model of Laguna City differ from those in the model of South Horizons, some variables which have effective influence in the South Horizons are not applicable in the Laguna City. The reasons for the exclusions will be explained later.

Excluded variables

DISTT and DISTS are both internal locational variables and are excluded. This implies they have little influence on the unit price. Their absolute t-value are respectively 1.270 and 1.164. They are insignificant in affecting the unit price.

The reason for the DISTT not to be significant in affecting the unit price is not the same as in the South Horizons. As the choice of transportation node (t-node) development is based on the issues of convenience, effectiveness and the efficiency of the type of transportation, so bus terminal is then selected to be the t-node for South Horizons and the MTR station to be the t-node for Laguna City.

During the process of map analysis, it is found that there is a long distance between the t-node and the estate when comparing with the distance difference in South Horizons.[9] The necessary walking distance from the Lam Tin MTR station (Sin Fat Road Exit) to the entrance of the Laguna City is about 370 metres, This distance is the summation of three sections of path. They include the Sin Fat Road section, two sections of covered walkways constructed by the developers.

Since there is such a distance to pass before entering the development, the internal difference between the furthest block and the nearest block is comparatively small. It may be argued that people could utilize the entry point as the reference of measurement rather than the Sin Fat Road MTR exit. It seems to be a possible way in contrasting the difference among the internal distance from each block. Nevertheless, it is not reasonable as there is an actual walking distance between the MTR exit to the entrance point of the development. A person may find the walking distance from the entry point to his home block is less crucial when he has walked for a reasonably long way. A dollar-worth candy means a lot difference to a boy with one dollar in pocket than to a billionaire.

In respect to the physical variables, all the orientation dummy variables (ORIS, ORIW and ORIN) are being excluded from the model. The absolute t-value for ORIS, ORIW and ORIN are 0.027, 0.739 and 0.560 respectively, which are far away from the critical

---

[9] The bus terminal is right situated within the estate.

value of about 2. Therefore they have very few significance in affecting the unit price within the Laguna City.

The result can be justified by the layout design. Similar to the South Horizons, the design layout of blocks in Laguna City is also "diamond shape." This design makes it possible for every unit to have frontages bearing at least two orientations. For example, referring to the floor plan, Flat A in Block 1 is classified as north orientated in the model. The directions of the view available are north-east (the living room) and north-west (the bedroom).

Apart from the layout design the distribution of the whole estate contribute to the result, too. Unlike South Horizons, Laguna City is comparatively packed. It can be easily observed that most of the units are shielded by the other blocks. This situation is even worst for the blocks located at the central part of the development.

For those which are not located at the central part of the development, that is on the fringe, or peripheral area, the influence by the orientation is being cancelled out. This cancellation can be illustrated by the following example. Assume residents prefer to capture a higher solar amount, Flat A and H in Block 1 to Block 12 shall have a higher unit price. It is because these units are not shielded by the other blocks. On the other hand, Flat D and E in Block 29 to Block 31 and Block 33 to Block 38 shall have a higher unit price, too. As a result, the effect in increasing the unit price is cancelled off by each other when the price data from the mentioned blocks are utilized at the same time. Since there are hundreds of transaction records in the data pool covering every block within the Laguna City development are computed, this "calling off" effect shall apply.

The LOSS variable is also excluded from the model, the absolute t-value of the LOSS variable is 1.149. The implication for this exclusion is that the loss ratio is not critical on affecting the unit price. The result is not as same as in the South Horizons. The reason for the difference is that the loss ratio in relatively small in Laguna City. Besides, they have almost the same value[10]

---

[10] LOSS ranged from 0.16 to 0.22.

purchaser would find little difference in the loss ratio among
different units. The deduction in price is implicitly borne in their
consideration.

Physical Variables

Generally speaking, AGE, GROSS and VERT performed well in
the model for Laguna City as expected. They are the three physical variables which remained in the model. They are found to
be highly significant to the unit price in the model.

In the SPSS results, the variable, AGE, achieved an absolute
t-value of 9.928 and a coefficient of 14.46. This implies that this
variable is very highly significant in the determination of unit
price. Moreover, the coefficient shows that the unit price will
have a drop of about HK$14.50 if the property transacted is a
month older.

This decline rate appears to be even higher than the one in
South Horizons. Notwithstanding higher face values, it could be
that the rates of depreciation for the two developments are very
close since the mean unit price for Laguna City is higher than
the one for South Horizons.

The variable GROSS is another physical variable which
remained in the model. It was found to be highly significant,
too. The absolute t-value for GROSS is 8.381 and its coefficient
is 0.537. This implies that unit price would increase by about
HK$0.54 when there is an increase of one square foot in the
gross floor area of the unit. If the gross floor area of a property
increases from 639 square feet to 961 square feet, the unit price
would increase only by about HK$173. As with South Horizons,
the difference in unit price is relatively small. The price difference
is even smaller in the Laguna City development, but the effect
is significant.

The last physical variable is VERT. VERT bears an absolute
t-value of 4.508 and a coefficient at 500.18. The variable VERT
is also significant in the determination of unit price. The coefficient value implies that the unit price will be raised by HK$500.18
if the subject property is taken from the first floor to the top
floor.

Since the total number of storeys for the buildings in Laguna

City ranges from 25 to 28, it is calculated that the mean is about 26.67 for the data input. Assuming the function is perfectly linear and the difference is the same, the increment will be approximately HK$19.00 for each rise of one storey. Again, the calculation unit should be in vertical ratio if precision is required.

The rate of increase in price appears to be higher than that in South Horizons. The compactness and dense distribution of the estate may account for the difference. It becomes more critical to have a longer solar period and better view if there is a rise in the vertical ratio. In South Horizons, it makes less difference as the rate of change in solar period and the quality of view change is relatively lower for a less compact development.

Time variable

The coefficient value of the time variable, TIME, is –59.87. It has a high absolute t-value of 5.40 showing its significance. As with the South Horizons model, the negative sign in the coefficient has confirmed the downward trend in capital value during the period from 15 November, 1994 to 15 November, 1995, after the government imposed the anti-speculation measures, when both the price and the transaction volume of the residential property market cooled down. The unit price would have declined by HK$59.87 monthly within the period. The results reflect the real situation the residential property market in that period.

The decline rate in Laguna City is higher than that in South Horizons. We should, however, remember that the mean unit price in Laguna City is also higher than in South Horizons.[11] If the decline rate is measured as a percentage, the decline rate will be about 1.2% for Laguna City and 0.8% for South Horizons. The real difference is actually insignificant.

Comparison on Determinants of Unit Price between South Horizons and Laguna City

The model for South Horizons explains empirically over 97.98%

---

[11] Refer to Table 1 and Table 2.

of the variation in the unit price by independent variables. Also, most variables have shown their expected effects on the unit price in both developments. It has been empirically proven that AGE, VERT and TIME have identical effects on the change in unit prices in both developments.

Regarding the magnitude of the coefficient, it is found that the absolute magnitude of coefficient in Laguna City is higher than in South Horizons. This phenomenon can be explained by the empirical difference in their unit price. Unit price is generally 5% higher in Laguna City. Therefore, it is reasonable to expect that the magnitude of variation in Laguna City is higher to a certain extent. Some of these variables are, however, very significant in the model of South Horizons.

For variables such as DISTT and the orientation dummies, the empirical insignificance is due to some technical problems in the process of regression analysis, for instance, the counter-effect created in the orientation variables in the case of Laguna City.

Nevertheless, it cannot be denied that there are some factors which can cause failures in the model. In other words, the model may not be universally applicable to all kinds of comprehensive development. Therefore, people should apply the model with extra care and with understanding of its constraints.

The factors which affect the effectiveness of the model include the layout design, compactness and the insolation of the development. Laguna City is a denser and compact development with closer proximity to the neighbouring development when comparing with South Horizons.

The layout design and the compactness in Laguna city makes the orientation insignificant in the unit price determination. In addition, the dependence on other nearby developments causes the shopping arcade within the estate to become less important.

We can observe from above that even for similar types of residential development, there are differences in the determination of the unit prices. From the point of developer, mere comparison of market prices may not provide the best estimation of market potential of the site. With the advent of the super computer, it is becoming easier and easier to produce good forecasting results provided that the input source is reliable. With a reliable database, it is therefore not difficult to estimate the extent to which the property prices are affected by market variables.

Application of Regression Analysis on Land Market — A Tale of Two Cities

For anyone who has visited both Taipei and Shanghai, it may be a striking surprise to them that despite the political complexion between the two systems, there are a lot of similarities in the atmosphere at the local level such as the similar local culture, similar character of local shops and similar local traffic chaos, which are all so different from the third major Chinese city (in terms of economic development), Hong Kong.

What this examination tries to deduce is the difference in the factors that determine the market land prices in Shanghai city and Taipei city. Hong Kong is not included in this study because the city area is relatively small and the market itself is relatively efficient. To this extent, the application of hedonic pricing model may not be that easy to be tested.

Shanghai is the major land market in mainland China with an average annual land sale record of more than 300 pieces of land since 1992 (Li, 1996). This is one of the booming real estate markets in mainland China with a huge hinterland in the eastern side of the city, Pudong area, for development. Investment funds from overseas, particularly from Hong Kong and other Asian countries are astronomical. However, due to the oversupply, especially in the office market, rentals start to stabilize recently. On the other hand, after years of rocketing land prices in the 1980s (an average of 18.7% rise in land prices in Taipei between 1978 to 1987 [Han, et al., 1992]), market activities started to slow down with a stabilized land price level. However, with the completion of a number of infrastructure projects such as the mass transit system, land prices in some locality are still on the rising trend. Despite the worldwide economic slow down, Taiwan still maintains a very high foreign exchange reserves and a strong economy.

Hence, we have two cities with very similar cultural and social background one is taking off and there other is stabilizing. If the determinants of land prices are the same everywhere given an active market, then the degree to which these two cities are influenced by these determinants could be very similar, unless the socio-political system has distorted the market operation to a certain degree. This will be examined by the comparison of the results. A tale of land market and policy of these two cities will then be told at the end.

Methodology

The examination here is based on a research done by Han, et al. in 1992 on the determination of land price in Taipei city and a similar research by the author, followed by a comparison of the factors generated in the regression analyses that are considered to be important in the determination of land prices in these two cities. But first of all, let us look at the fundamentals of the determination of land prices in a market economy which can be served as a benchmark for the comparison.

M. H. Yeates (1965) has done a classic research on the examination of the spatial distribution of Chicago land prices over a period of 50 years. He consolidates a number of other similar researches as well as classical theory of land price. One of his objectives is to test the validity of the established theory of the factors affecting land prices, especially distance from the CBD.

According to Yeates, conclusions from various researches on the effect of distance from CBD as well as major commercial areas produce contradictory results. Some substantiate the assumption that distance from the CBD does affect land prices, while others reject such a notion. Yeates explains that such differences in results may be attributed to the surrogate for land price used. While some used assessed evaluations, others used the average price for single family dwelling units in a block which includes both the prices of land and of improvement.

He also notes in the relationship between land prices and population densities that if there is a negative relationship between land prices and distance from the centre of the city and, if population densities decrease with the distance from the centre of the city, then land prices and population densities should be positively related but such relationship may be affected by the changing characteristics of the urban population such as the racial component.

In general, we can conclude from Yeates' findings that:

i) the influence of CBD in Chicago is decreasing while the potential of different "growth sector" within the city is increasing;

ii) because of (i), the importance of distance from CBD is also diminishing in the determination of land prices;

iii) distance to regional service centres is only important to land prices in high-income non-white regions, but could be detrimental in old areas of manufacturing and commerce areas occupied by the low-income non-white population.

iv) the influence of recreational and physical amenities (in this case the mean distance from Lake Michigan) on land prices is gaining significance;

v) within the city, high speed low-cost transport facilities are no longer important determinants of land prices;

vi) as the percentage of non-white population in an area increases, land prices decrease, until such time as the population density in this area begins to rise, at which time land prices start to rise as a result of intense subdivision of property and competition for living space;

vii) finally, Yeates notes that the CBD will soon be complemented by a number of other foci which lie on and beyond the political limits of Chicago and their combined influence on land value structure may equal that of the core in the past.

A Tale of the Taipei Market

Based on market economic analysis of the determination of land prices, Han, et al. (1992) conduct an examination on behalf of the government on the factors affecting land prices in Taipei city. They build up a time series database of land prices from 1979–1990. However, it should be noted that in Taiwan, change in land ownership of land arising from market transaction activity is required to be registered with the local lands administration department. But there is no need to register the price of land. Nevertheless, in order to assess land taxes, the Taiwanese government has devised the "Public Announced Value" (PAV). The PAV is the land value assessed by the local lands administration department. It is frequently updated and revised. To this extent, it is taken by the researchers as the approximation of market land prices.

In addition, the researchers set out their objectives as to:

a) analyse the reasons behind the rise of land prices in Taiwan;
b) set up a model explaining the changes in land prices;
c) verify different land price theories; and
d) examine the relationship between land prices and such variables as population, land use as well as economy.

A total of 23 variables as having influence on land prices in Taiwan are stipulated under the following five main categories:

Population & Income	Finance	Taxes	Construction	Economic Indicators
Density	Bank deposit	Taxes collected	GFA	GNP growth
Working population	Bank loans	Capital gains tax	Building costs	rate
Household income	Interest rates	Land price tax	Length of roads	Exchange rate
Household expenses	Medium term rate	Conveyance tax	Area of roads	Saving rate
	M2 supply	Securities tax		Stock index
				CPI

Where:

Density: in the unit of thousand of people per sq. km. (denoted as DENSITY in the regression analysis)

Working population: working population over the age of 15, in the unit of one million people (denoted as LABOUR)

Household income: in the unit of 10,000 NTD (New Taiwan Dollar) (denoted as INCOME)

Household expenses: in the unit of 10,000 NTD (denoted as EXPENSE)

Bank deposit: including all financial institutions, in the unit of 100 billion NTD (denoted as DEPOSIT)

Bank loans: including all financial institutions, in the unit of 100 billion NTD (denoted as LOAN)

Interest rates:	average annual interest rate for fixed deposit (denoted as DRATE)
Medium term rate:	medium to long term interest rate for bank loan (denoted as LRATE)
M2 supply:	central bank M2 money supply annual growth rate (denoted as M2)
Taxes collected:	annual tax income by the government in the unit of 0.1 billion NTD (denoted as TAX)
Capital gains tax:	annual capital gains tax in the unit of 0.1 billion NTD (denoted as ILAND)
Land price tax:	annual tax income on land value in the unit of 0.1 billion NTD (denoted as PLAND)
Conveyance tax:	annual tax income on conveyance deeds in the unit of 0.1 billion NTD (denoted as DEED)
Securities tax:	annual tax income on stock exchange in the unit of 0.1 billion NTD (denoted as BOND)
GFA:	gross built-up areas in the city in the unit of ha. (denoted as BUILD)
Building costs:	gross construction costs of all built-up areas in the unit of 0.1 billion NTD (denoted as VALUE)
Length of roads:	total length of all roads in the city in the unit of km (denoted as LENGTH)
Area of roads:	total areas of all roads in the city in the unit of ha. (denoted as AREA)
GNP growth rate:	annual GNP growth rate (denoted as GROWTH)
Exchange rate:	exchange rate between US dollar and NTD (denoted as EXCHANGE)
Saving rate:	annual saving rate in the deposit accounts (denoted as SAVE)
Stock index:	Taiwan Stock Exchange index (denoted as STOCK)
CPI:	consumer price index with 1981 as base year (denoted as PINDEX)

By carrying out a stepwise regression procedure, relevant variables are entered into the model and less influential variables are sifted out. Accordingly, they conclude from their analysis that:

a) The relationship between population density and land prices is not very high;

b) As far as income is concerned, only the deposit rate shows a positive relation with land prices;

c) Different variables in the economic indicators group give different results. If GNP is removed from the model, the stock index produces a negative relationship with land prices. This, according to the authors, shows that the stock market and the land or property market are competitors for investment funds. A similar negative relationship appears for the M2 money supply variable. And, predictably, CPI has a positive relationship with land prices, meaning land is a good investment to hedge against inflation.

d) Tax variables show a positive relationship with land prices. The explanation of this by the authors is that a rise in land taxes will increase the land costs in transaction and hence increase land price. However, this should be subject to further analysis of elasticity of demand for land in Taiwan before such a conclusion can be made. Although land is more or less physically fixed, land uses can be flexible, and accordingly, Henry George's notion of 100% land tax (George, 1898) is not acceptable.

e) Contrary to traditional valuation theory that the lower the interest rate the higher the property price, the results of the test on interest rates show a positive relations with land price in Taiwan meaning a rise in interest rates will cause a rise in land price. This conclusion can be attributed to two different reasons: firstly, a rise in interest rates represents a rise in expected inflation and hence demand for real property increases. Secondly, such a conclusion can also be the result of the interaction of interest rate variables with other variables in the regression model. This is subject to further examination.

f) Finally, both the length and area of roads show a positive relationship with land prices.

A Tale of the Shanghai Market

In this analysis of the Shanghai land market, transactions of land use rights in Shanghai were recorded by the Shanghai Authority for the period 1988 to date, although only the 1992–1993 transactions have been made public with details. The dependent variable for the test is described as follows:

$$\text{Market Price} = \frac{\text{Total Market Price for Land Use Rights}}{\text{Site Area}}$$

In the public records of market land prices, the official records only show land prices in the unit of accommodation value (which is land price divided by gross floor area of the project). Hence, to compare the two cities on the same basis, the accommodation value will be converted into total land price first and then to unit land price based on the above equation. In addition, since the land use rights reform in mainland China only allows for the sale of the leasehold interest of land or the so-called land use rights (Walker and Li, 1994), the term "land use rights" is used here as a proxy of land in the case of Taipei.

The predictor variables

A total of 18 predictor variables have been identified and are drawn from the conclusions of the various similar research studies, which area also thought to be comparable with the predictor variables used in the Taipei study. These variables are:

1) **Comland** represents the % of land in the respective urban district (a total of ten urban districts in Shanghai excluding Pudong new area) used for commercial purpose as surveyed by the Planning Science and Technology Office of the Shanghai Land Administrative Bureau in Summer, 1992. The inclusion of this variable in the regression analysis is to examine the effect of the legacy of the old land use pattern created under the planned allocation of land on the decision of developers under the land use rights reform.

2) **Resland** represents the % of land in the respective urban district used for residential purpose as surveyed by the Planning Science and Technology Office of the Shanghai Land Administrative Bureau in Summer, 1992.

3) **Indland** represents the % of land in the respective urban district used for industrial purpose as surveyed by the Planning Science and Technology Office of the Shanghai Land Administrative Bureau in Summer, 1992.

4) **Employ** represents the % increase in 1992 (over 1991) in the number of employees employed in private enterprises in the respective urban district in which the site is located. This variable relates to the local economy (district by district) since private enterprises are supposed to be more market oriented so that the more people employed in the private enterprises in a particular district, the higher the demand for premises by these enterprises and their employees.

5) **Newjvs** represents the % of joint ventures set up in the respective urban district compared to the total joint ventures set up in the whole city in 1992.

6) **Grade** represents the land grade as classified by the Shanghai city government in the respective urban district, in which the site is located. There are a total of five grades of land covering the whole urban Shanghai Municipality. To avoid distortion problem noted by Gunst and Mason (1980) that could possibly occur when more than two choices are available for one dummy variable, five dummy variables are used instead just one variable for the predictor "land grade." Hence, there are Grade 1, Grade 2, Grade 3, Grade 4 and Grade 5. For instance, when the particular site locates in Grade 3 land, instead of giving this variable a number "3," the variable of Grade 3 becomes 1, while those for the four become 0s.

7) **Hirise** represents the % of high rise buildings (those buildings over 20 floors) in terms of GFA out of the total built-up GFA in the respective urban district in which the site locates. This variable tends to examine the effect of the existing development density in the particular district on land price.

8) **Popden** represents the population density per sq. km in the respective urban district in which the site is located.

9) **Size** is the size of the site in sq. metres.

10) A dummy variable is used for **Use Type 1** as mixed office and high class residential use buildings as this is the main type of development project that attracts foreign developers and investors, while **Use Type 2** is for pure residential development.

11) **Distance** in km of the site from the Bund which is taken as a representation of the CBD area in Shanghai.

12) **PR** is the plot ratio allowed on the respective site.

13) **Chousing** is the GFA of housing built in 1992 for open market trading.

14) **Indout** is the percentage increase of industrial output over 1991 in the respective urban district in the city.

15) **Term** refers to the length of the leasehold interest. Normally, a term of 50 years is given for commercial projects and 70 years for residential projects.

16) **Office** refers to the percentage of total built-up office space in the city found in the respective district.

17) **Retail** refers to the percentage of total built-up retail space in the city found in the respective district.

18) **Stock** refers to the index of all B-share stocks in the Shanghai Stock Exchange. B-shares are the shares available to all investors inside and outside China.

Again, a stepwise regression analysis is carried out based on these 18 variables. It is shown that only six out of the eighteen variables are found to be significantly affecting the determination of land prices in Shanghai. Following traditional wisdom, distance to CBD has a significant negative effect on land price in Shanghai. Hence, the farther away from the Bund, or the CBD, the less expensive the land price becomes. In addition, population density also poses as a significant negative factor affecting land price. This is quite obvious given the dense population in Shanghai.

It is also found that land prices are positively sensitive to the percentage of commercial land in the district. The higher the percentage of land used for commercial purpose, the higher the land prices in that district. For site specific variables, land prices are sensitive to the prime location of grade one land. But quite interestingly, for other grades in the city, land prices are indifferent to them. Finally, land prices are very significantly affected by the plot ratio (or the ratio between gross floor area allowed and site area). This is not surprising as the higher the plot ratio allowed on site, the higher the gross floor area to be built and the higher the income to be generated, and naturally the higher the land price. Finally, for the similar reason, the larger the site area the higher the land price.

A Tale of the Two Cities

Table 6 below produces a summary of the results of the two empirical tests.

Table 6 Comparison of the Determinants of Land Prices in Shanghai and Taipei

	Shanghai			Taipei		
	Variables	B	T	Variables	B	T
	COMLAND	0.175143	3.05	LOAN	324.3057	10.252
	DISTANCE	−0.270342	−4.145	DRATE	574.0162	4.733
	G1	0.328244	2.481	LRATE	2479.5337	15.206
	POPDEN	−0.198299	−2.036	ILAND	149.3522	8.463
	PR	0.993718	20.869	STOCK	−2.8629	−26.769
	SIZE	0.092146	3.128	SAVE	247.1045	2.177
Adjusted R^2 = 0.824						
Adjusted R^2 = 0.9078				0.9969		

The comparison between the Shanghai land market and the Taipei land market can be made by looking at the adjusted R^2 in Shanghai and R^2 in Taipei. R^2 is basically the coefficient of determination. It shows the extent to which the factors included in the equation can explain the fluctuation of the land prices. In both cases, there is at lease 90% of the fluctuation of the data can be explained by the variables selected by the stepwise model. This implies that we are able to identify to a large extent the major predictor variables in the two cities.

A further examination can also be made in the behaviour of the predictor variables. First of all, the traditional notion that land price decreases with distance from the CBD is only validated in the Shanghai market. For Taipei, since the variable is not included in the analysis, there is no way to find out. However, as a proxy, the researchers in the report also carry out similar regression analyses for other cities in Taiwan with the distance variable. It is found out that proximity to public transport terminals does not have a substantial effects on land prices in Taiwan. However, the product of the distance to CBD and the distance to a public bus stop has a negative relation meaning the shorter distance to such a combination, the higher the land price.

Market land prices in Shanghai have a significant positive relationship with the distribution of land for commercial use which is not found in the Taipei study. In terms of the relationship with population density, market land prices in Shanghai shows a significant negative relationship while there is no effect in Taipei.

Furthermore, land prices in Taipei are very sensitive to the changes in such financial and economic indicators as the interest rates, saving rate (capital for investment) and performance in the stock market (which is in competition with the land market as the negative relationship shows), while the Shanghai land market is not.

Having examined the comparison between the two cities, we can, in general, draw an interesting deduction from the above. In the examination of the Shanghai market, there is a limitation in the data as the time series only last for two years. It may not be the representative enough for the examination of the whole picture of the market. However, as the market mechanism only started to become active after 1991, it does provide a forum for the examination of a market in the infancy. It seems quite clear that when a land market starts to develop, the environmental factors such as population density and characteristics of the site account for a very important role in determining land prices. In addition, location and distance from the city centre are also important variables. Location in particular refers to prime location only as the city is yet to develop and there is little differentiation between other grades than first grade land.

In addition, as land development take some time to accomplish, the existing land use system will become a constraint to land development in the short term. Moreover, in a transforming socialist land market, commercial sector of real estate normally flourishes more easily than other sectors such as housing as the commercial sector involves less social welfare contention. Since office demand is usually high because of prolonged under-supply in an infant real estate market with prominent growth potential such as Shanghai, the locality with a higher content of commercial land distribution will therefore naturally draw a higher demand from prospective developers and investors.

All these factors correlate tightly with traditional analysis of land price behaviour and location theories where physical environment of the site determines to a large extent the price of land. The analysis in the Shanghai market shows that once market activities start to generate, these factors begin to operate even the market is in transition from a planned economic entity. When the market has become more sophisticated and developed, market behaviour proceed to the next stage and some of these traditional factors fade away and replaced by modern economic and financial variables such as those found in the Taipei model.

In the Taipei analysis, we found that when a land market has become more mature, land acquires the role of a financial asset, apart from a major input in the urban development. Because of its new role, investors, when pricing land and given their own investment portfolio, will look at the normal financial and economic indicators that are normally applied in the assessment of asset values. Such indicators include interest rates and performance in other investment markets. This view also coincides with the modern view of the determination of land prices that is being developed recently. Hence, with a much more developed economy, physical environmental factors become less important, for instance information technology renders physical distance between people less crucial.

Consequently, when we look at the emerging land markets with similar backgrounds, such as the markets in Asia, it may not be difficult to develop a progressing trend by which we can identify the various crucial factors affecting the market mechanism according to the stage in which the market is currently experiencing and to predict the other influential factors when this market proceeds into a further stage. It will therefore be interesting if further research work can be extended to other markets in the European and American continents to examine if such a trend does exist. If the results coincide with the above, we may be able to establish that factors affecting land price determination do vary with the development of the whole macro economy.

Summary

We should emphasize here that D.C.F. is no panacea for the problems in accurate development appraisal. The logic of D.C.F. is basically the same as in the residual model, with a starting point of an estimate of the gross development value and with various cost items deducted at various points of time. It is noted from the examples above that the D.C.F. model applied in these cases is still very simplified. In all these cases, payment to various agents are made at standard intervals. This is done on purpose to show the versatility of the model to cope with various payment schedules. The model applied in these examples is a sample only and should only be used with variations in the assumptions due to changes in circumstances.

By the same token, the assumption that development takes two years to complete may not be realistic for most development projects, especially those with problems in their foundations which is common in Hong Kong. But with the application of a powerful computer, these assumptions can always be modified according to the needs of an individual project to deal with any major problems.

On the other hand, the use of D.C.F. in development appraisal does provide the analyst with more options in examining the feasibility of the project, which is more important to the developer/investor than just knowing the value of the site.

With the development of various price forecasting models we have seen in this chapter, there is no reason to the application of a more scientific/financial based development appraisal model in Hong Kong in the future, when the market itself get more mature and sophisticated.

Chapter 5

Conclusion

In the previous chapters, we have briefly discussed the theoretical importance of distinguishing between value and price. Such a distinction is needed at the theoretical level as development appraisal should aim at assessing land value rather than price, especially during periods of excessive speculation. In times of excessive speculation, market prices only indicate the current short term sentiment of the most probable price, but not the worth of the real estate. In the appraisal of land value, this is even more important as land value is in the form of residual value which is determined by the value that the land user can expect to gain from developing the site. Hence, in the broadest sense, land itself should not command a cost figure as there is no cost for the existence of land (except improvement of land such as infrastructure).

With this residual nature of land value, one will have to start from the assessment of the asset value of the completed development. In this respect, there are basically two ways of determining real estate value. When the market is active enough and most of the transactions are conducted by way of sales within a very close period, valuation by way of market comparison provides a quick and relatively reliable way of determining real estate value. However, when the development is built for investment purposes, i.e. for rental income, determination of the value of real estate based on income capitalization, or the investment approach, will be more appropriate. This is normally the case when the development is commercial where tenancy agreement is less biased towards the protection of tenant than in the case of residential properties. Moreover, a number of institutional investors such as insurance companies are always in search of good quality income producing properties as they have financial commitments to pay out cash periodically. In addition, the supply of good tenants in the office market is also relatively abundant compared to other sectors. Hence, rental data does provide a reliable reflection of the market demand and supply situation.

However, in the operational mechanism of the investment approach, there are two schools of thought. On the one hand, the traditional approach regards current market data as the only reliable source of information. As no one can forecast with a hundred percent certainty about the future, we might as well not do any forecasting at all. The only data that could be juggled around is the market capitalization yield. But it is exactly this issue that creates problem for this approach. We have seen that in the traditional term and reversion approach, which is the dominant approach in the UK property profession, the use of the market yield, instead of rate of return or discount rate to discount a fixed stream of incomes is justified by the fact that the reversion is under-valued as the current open market rent is assumed to be fixed until the point of reversion. This however is only true if the term is short, inflationary effect is weak and future cash flow patterns is relatively less risky from the point of the investors, which is normally not the case.

In cases where the investor wants a higher compensation for cash income receivable in the future and rental movement seems to be fluctuating cyclically, the application of the D.C.F. model, which is the second school with heavy emphasis on the financial analysis of cash flow patterns, is more appropriate. There is basically no major difference in the logic of the D.C.F. model which tries to assess the value of the asset by looking at the total discounted values of all the future income flows. The major improvement of the D.C.F. model is to build in all the foreseeable fluctuations in the market with the most accurate possible forecasts. We can therefore assume that rental will go up at various growth rates as well as decrease at various rates in the future. In addition, we can even have various discount rates to reflect the investor's perception of risk at various stages in the future. It may be argued that forecasting is only as good as a wild guess. If there is enough market information, there are a lot of forecasting models available from management science and financial studies that could be employed in simple analysis of the variables in the D.C.F. model. Just because it is difficult to have accurate forecasting does not constitute a good excuse for not doing it at all.

Once the value of the completed development is determined, all the development costs, developer's profit, interest payments and legal charges on land will be deducted from it leaving the residual value of the land. This makes a logical flow of events as there are no other claimants on this residual amount other than land itself. As a result, land value always depends on the expectation of the gross development value, which is a function of the demand and supply factors in the property market. This may provide a theoretical counter-argument against the claim that increase in land price leads to increase in property price and hence that the government is at fault to foster a "high-land-price" policy. This "high-land-price" policy is only true when the market is assessing land value by comparing the latest land sale records only rather than looking at the affordability of the property market. However, land is different from property in the sense that the degree of homogeneity of residential flats in a big development is much higher than that of two pieces of adjoining land. In addition, the rate of market transaction of land is much less frequent than that of the property market.

It is only when a market is in a very active state and the market size is relatively small that comparison of market land transaction records could provide enough information for the appraisal of land. Hong Kong's land market is one of these efficient and small markets which makes development appraisal nothing more than a simple comparison of market transaction records. This, however, does not exclude the use of more analytical approach in the process of development appraisal which can provide a much longer term consideration of the development potential of land.

The land market in Hong Kong is the best example in the world to show the combination of a socialist land tenure system within a capitalist economy. With one of the best-known free economies in the world, the government keeps a very strict control on the land ownership system by selling only land leases to developers. The importance of the revenue from land sales to the Hong Kong government's income is well-understood. One of the reasons for this active land market is that most of the land (or more accurately the long leases on land) is sold under the public auction system which makes market information on the demand and supply of land more readily available. In addition, land sold through government auction normally carries a certain degree of development control which allows the government to monitor a better macro land use system in Hong Kong.

On the other hand, these development controls and conditions are not too rigid to react to changes in the macroeconomic environment. There is a mechanism through which the land owner or prospective purchaser of land can apply for modifications of one or more of the lease conditions. One of the most common types of modification is the change of use due to change in the economic environment. In most of these modification cases, if granted, there will be a need to pay a land premium by the applicant to the government. The logic is that if the modification of the lease conditions will lead to an enhancement of land value for the applicant, then the applicant should repay the sum of the resulting capital gains to the public.

Consequently, a central issue in the development appraisal is the reliability of the appraisal model. We have given a brief discussion on the various appraisal models of real estate and a more in-depth analysis of the appraisal models of land. In principle, the value of any real estate is the summation of the future income in present day value terms. This is the basic view. On this foundation, there are generally two mainstream models for development appraisal of land. The first one is the traditional residual valuation model which looks at land value as a straight line deduction of costs and profit from the gross development value without considering the cash flow pattern during the development period. The argument for this appraisal model is that it is simple and fast. In fact, in Hong Kong, all the developer needs is a quick guideline as market information on land price is quite readily available and land transactions occur quite frequently.

However, one should also bear in mind that land development, from a developer's / investor's point of view, is after all a business. Like any other businesses, the focus should be on cash flow patterns. This is also one of the reasons why in the US, where basically everything is treated as a business, the teaching of real estate is incorporated in the department of finance or business administration rather than having a separate department of property. The second mainstream development appraisal model therefore looks at the analysis of cash flow in the future, but discounted at the specified rate of return to reflect the common basis of present value. The discounted cash flow model, or in the short form D.C.F., allows the developer/investor to look at the life cycle of the investment in a numerical format. As a result, it has the capacity of incorporating any changes in the assumptions concerning cash flow (both inflows and outflows) in the future. This is a direct contrast to the traditional residual valuation where a single payment made at the completion of the project is assumed. We all understand that the payment pattern in the construction industry is more often than not made in instalments rather than as a single payment. The D.C.F. model is therefore more realistic.

Despite the obvious advantages of the D.C.F. model, there is a certain degree of resistance in moving towards complete D.C.F.-based development appraisal in Hong Kong. One of the major arguments for this is that since the real estate market in Hong Kong is very active and transaction records are basically available to the public fairly quickly after the completion of sale, there is therefore no need for an in-depth analytical element to be incorporated in the appraisal model. All is needed in the development appraisal is therefore a quick guide of the current market situation, and this is what the traditional model does best.

Besides, although the traditional development appraisal model concentrates on current date market information such as construction costs and price levels, these reflect actual market information. In the D.C.F. model, there is a lot of forecasting to be conducted in order to make it sensible. As nobody can guarantee a hundred percent reliable forecast, there is always a "garbage-in-garbage-out" problem in the D.C.F. model.

Nevertheless, the choice for the development appraisal model in the future is obvious. The traditional model is easy and reliable in current market information, but it is logically flawed. The alternative, D.C.F. model, is more realistic but deficient in reliable information forecasting. We can always improve, amend and strengthen a model that is deficient, but not necessarily when the model is flawed. For the forecasting weakness, there are already some statistical models such as multiple regression analysis as well as simulation models that are designed for better forecasting results. In addition, the advancement in computer technology makes number crunching a much easier exercise for the analyst. There is therefore no excuse for not at least trying to apply a more scientific model in the development appraisal of land when other investment markets, such as the capital markets, have already accepted such models as a norm in the investment decision process.

Moreover, in the long term development of the land market, Hong Kong is becoming part of a much larger market, the China land market, developers will have to examine their business strategy in a portfolio dimension such that they will have to consider the cash flow patterns in other markets in China which are still relatively less efficient than in Hong Kong. The application of the D.C.F. model can have the bonus that it will force the developer to examine the various elements in the development process that affect cash flow more carefully than just applying a rule of thumb as more variables will creep in when the other land markets in China are being considered together. In this respect, there is no reason why we should not familiarize ourselves with the logic of the modern development appraisal models so that some specific version may be designed for the application in this growing land market in the world economy.

APPENDICES

Appendix 1 Land Auction Record in Hong Kong (1984–1996)

Date	Lot No.	Location	Use	Site Area (sq.f.)	Plot Ratio	Sale Price (HK$ m)	AV (HK$ psf)	Average Land Price (HK$ psf)
Government Land Auction Analysis								
18-Jan-84	NKIL 5982	Kowloon Bay Reclamation	Ind/Godown	44,294		17.8		402
18-Jan-84	STTL 248	Area 14B, Shatin	Ind/Godown	68,889		13.0		189
18-Jan-84	STTL 253	Area 41A, Shatin New Town	Residential	31,215		1.5		48
18-Jan-84	NKIL 5755	Lung Cheung Rd	Non-industrial	28,158		47.5		1,687
18-Jan-84	TMTL 264	Area 4C, Tuen Mun New Town	Residential	88,221		14.5		164
15-Feb-84	IL 8615	J/O Cotton Tree Drive & Queensway	Non-industrial	67,942		380.0		5,593
28-Feb-84	STTL 241	Area 14B, Sha Tin	Ind/Godown	226,796		36.4		160
28-Feb-84	TPTL 19	Area 4, Tai Po	Non-industrial	97,047		28.2		291
28-Feb-84	YLTL 423	Sai Ching St, Yuen Long	Non-industrial	39,202		15.1		385
28-Feb-84	TMTL 263	Area 4C, Tuen Mun New Town	Non-industrial	83,862		0.0		0
18-Apr-84	AIL 410	Aberdeen Main Rd	Non-industrial	16,996		56.0		3,295
18-Apr-84	STTL 254	Area 41A, Sha Tin New Town	Residential	15,737		0.9		54
18-Apr-84	CWIL 125	Kut Shing St., Chai Wan	Ind/Godown	39,719		32.0		806
30-Jul-84	L 99A	Tui Min Hoi, Sai Kung	Ind/Godown	22,088		0.0		0
30-Jul-84	CWIL 126	Ka Yip St, Chai Wan	Ind/Godown	15,069		0.0		0
30-Jul-84	IL 8618	J/O Queen's Rd C & Possession St	Non-industrial	12,658		35.0		2,765
30-Jul-84	KIL 10730	J/O Mody Rd & Science Museum Rd	Non-industrial	54,541		165.0		3,025
28-Nov-84	KIL 10729	Tsim Sha Tsui East	Non-industrial	30,677		190.0		6,194
28-Nov-84	NKIL 5998	Kowloon Bay Reclamation	Conc. Batching	22,152		30.0		1,354
28-Nov-84	STTL 271	Area 16B, Sha Tin New Town	In/Godown	23,681		3.9		163

Appendix 1 (Cont'd)

Date	Lot No.	Location	Use	Site Area	Plot Ratio	Sale Price	AV	Average Land Price
				(sq.f.)		(HK$ m)	(HK$ psf)	(HK$ psf)
Government Land Auction Analysis								
04-Feb-85	KIL 10742	547–555 Nathan Rd	Non-industrial	7,427		45.0		6,059
04-Feb-85	NKIL 5988	Yee Kuk St	Non-industrial	13,756		30.0		2,181
04-Feb-85	AIL 412	J/O Aberdeen Main Rd & Chengtu Rd	Non-industrial	5,786		27.0		4,667
04-Feb-85	STTL 274	Area 41A Shatin New Town	Residential	20,182		1.6		77
04-Feb-85	STTL 276	Area 14B, Shatin New Town	Ind/Godown	41,269		6.0		145
11-Mar-85	NKIL 6004	J/O Waterloo Rd & Lancashise Rd	Residential	30,602		20.0		654
18-Apr-85	IL 8571	Queensway	Non-industrial	115,066		703.0		6,110
18-Apr-85	STTL 225	Area 41A, Sha Tin New Town	Residential	102,419		27.0		264
18-Apr-85	STTL 194	Area 41A Sha Tin New Town	Residential	126,045		45.5		361
18-Apr-85	STTL 252	Area 41A, Sha Tin New Town	Residential	10,333		1.8		174
18-Apr-85	STTL 275	Area 14B, Sha Tin New Town	Ind/Godown	52,905		12.1		229
20-May-85	STTL 279	Area 41A, Sha Tin New Town	Residential	424,529		138.0		325
20-May-85	STTL 247	Area 14B, Sha Tin New Town	Ind/Godown	36,285		9.2		254
20-May-85	IL 8633	Harbour Rd, Wanchai	Commercial	36,909		302.0		8,182
20-May-85	RBL 1061	South Bay Rd, Repulse Bay	Residential	39,288		76.0		1,934
20-May-85	IL 8628	Moorsom Rd, Jardines' Lookout	Residential	2,616		51.0		19,498
20-May-85	IL 8678	Sai Ning Street, Kennedy Town	Non-industrial	7,319		25.5		3,484
20-May-85	IL 8621	Victoria Rd, Kennedy Town	Ind/Godown	5,382		9.0		1,672
24-Sep-85	TMTL 235	Area 11, Tuen Mun New Town	Non-industrial	38,233		30.0		785
24-Sep-85	CWIL 124	Kut Shing St, Chai Wan	Ind/Godown	7,247		7.1		980
24-Sep-85	SOIL 95	Shek O Village	Residential	985		0.5		508

Date	Lot	Location	Type			
24-Sep-85	NKIL 6012	Poplar St	Non-industrial	1,241	2.8	2,256
24-Sep-85	KIL 10751	Tai Nan St	Non-industrial	898	1.6	1,782
24-Sep-85	NKIL 5972	Kowloon Bay	Ind/Godown	16,103	14.9	925
24-Oct-85	KIL 10722	Canton Rd, Tsim Sha Tsui	Non-industrial	69,416	636.0	9,162
19-Nov-85	KIL 10726	94-96 Waterloo Rd	Residential	17,599	60.0	3,409
19-Nov-85	CWIL 126	Ka Yip St, Chai Wan	Ind/Godown	15,069	0.0	0
12-Dec-85	TYTL 92	Area 6, Tsing Yi	Ind/Godown	27,491	7.0	255
12-Dec-85	IL 8638	Albany Rd/Robinson Rd	Residential	41,732	199.0	4,769
12-Dec-85	IL 8634	Kennedy Rd	Residential	8,625	55.0	6,377
12-Dec-85	CWIL 128	Kut Shing St, Chai Wan	Ind/Godown	16,372	14.7	898
23-Jan-86	KCTL 384	Tai Lin Pai Rd, Kwai Chung	Ind/Godown	17,976	14.3	796
23-Jan-86	L 1002	Tui Mui Hoi	Ind/Godown	34,778	6.1	175
23-Jan-86	STTL 261	Area 14B, Sha Tin New Town	Ind/Godown	143,698	36.0	251
23-Jan-86	RBL 1078	South Bay Rd, Repulse Bay	Residential	39,288	60.0	1,527
26-Feb-86	KIL 10874	94-96 Waterloo Rd	Residential	17,599	42.0	2,386
27-May-86	IL 8582	Supreme Court Rd	Non-industrial	173,837	1,005.0	5,781
26-Jun-86	SIL 798	382-384 Shau Kei Wan Rd	Non-industrial	1,302	3.2	2,457
26-Jun-86	KTIL 715	Kung Lik Rd, Dwun Tong	Residential	29,934	57.0	1,904
26-Jun-86	IL 8642	Sai Non-industrialng St, Kennedy Town	Ind/Godown	10,979	13.0	1,184
26-Sep-86	KIL 10795	2 Forfar Rd, Kowloon City	Residential	34,692	83.0	2,392
26-Sep-86	KIL 10796	165 Argyle St	Residential	16,490	31.0	1,880
26-Sep-86	SIL 799	352-354, Shau Kei Wan Rd	Non-industrial	1,322	3.2	2,421
29-Oct-86	IL 8653	Lockhard Rd	Non-industrial	5,451	65.0	11,925
29-Oct-86	IL 8658	Hennessy Rd	Non-industrial	2,122	34.0	16,026
29-Oct-86	IL 8682	Sai Non-industrialng St, Kennedy Town	Non-industrial	7,922	39.0	4,923
29-Oct-86	L 5346	On Lok Tsuen, Fanling	Ind/Godown	21,840	6.0	275
29-Oct-86	L 5347	On Lok Tsuen, Fanling	Ind/Godown	18,191	5.0	275

Appendix 1 (Cont'd)

Date	Lot No.	Location	Use	Site Area (sq.f.)	Plot Ratio	Sale Price (HK$ m)	AV (HK$ psf)	Average Land Price (HK$ psf)
Government Land Auction Analysis								
19-Nov-86	IL 8681	New Market St	Non-industrial	1,431		3.1		2,167
19-Nov-86	SIL 800	Nam On St	Non-industrial	3,467		16.1		4,644
19-Nov-86	IL 8656	Tin Hau Temple Rd	Residential	165,549		645.0		3,896
18-Dec-86	IL 8655	258–262 Des Voeux Rd	Non-industrial	22,572		17.5		775
18-Dec-86	IL 8657	108–110 Des Voeux Rd West	Non-industrial	1,211		6.8		5,615
18-Dec-86	CWIL 132	Sheung On St	Ind/Godown	32,292		51.5		1,595
26-Feb-87	L 1008	Tui Min Hoi, Sai Kung	Ind/Godown	11,776		3.5		297
26-Feb-87	STTL 273	Area 14B, Sha Tin	Ind/Godown	60,278		41.0		680
23-Mar-87	CWIL 131	Sheung On St, Chai Wan	Ind/Godown	32,292		70.0		2,168
23-Mar-87	NKIL 6036	Kai Hing Rd, Kowloon Bay	Ind/Godown	59,062		125.0		2,116
23-Mar-87	L 1197	Razor Hill, Sai Kung	Residential	40,903		20.4		499
23-Mar-87	IL 8651	Wanchai Rd	Non-industrial	4,780		27.5		5,753
29-May-87	IL 8687	King's Rd	Ind/Godown	11,377		45.0		3,955
29-May-87	CWIL 134	Kai Yip St	Ind/Godown	34,445		83.0		2,410
29-May-87	IL 8667	Des Voeux Rd C	Non-industrial	22,583		840.0		37,197
24-Jun-87	NKIL 6040	Fung Shing St, Hammer Hill	Residential	60,278		169.0		2,804
24-Jun-87	NKIL 6032	Kai Fuk Rd; Kai Shing Rd, Kln Bay	Ind/Godown	258,334		0.0		0
24-Jun-87	STTL 282	Area 18B, Sha Tin	Ind/Godown	19,117		24.0		1,255
27-Jul-87	IL 8690	Tai Hang Drive	Residential	16,878		77.0		4,562
27-Jul-87	SSTL 37	Area 25, On Lok Tsuen, Fanling	Ind/Godown	10,195		10.3		1,010

Date	Lot	Location	Type				
28-Sep-87	SIL 83	Main St, Stanley	Non-ind.	1,615	12.1		7,494
28-Sep-87	RBL 1088	Mount Kellet Rd, Peak	Residential	64,067	53.0		827
28-Sep-87	FS/STTL 17	Fanling	Ind	36,296	28.0		771
26-Oct-87	IL 8688	Old Peak Road	Residential	61,602	500.0		8,117
26-Oct-87	NKIL 6043	Hing Wah Street, Cheung Sha Wan	Comm/Carpark	16,361	168.0		10,268
26-Oct-87	FSSTL 14	On Lok Tsuen, Fanling	Ind/Godown	11,743	8.7		741
27-Nov-87	NKIL 6032	Kai Fuk Road, Kowloon Bay	Ind/Godown	239,131	470.0		1,965
27-Nov-87	FSSTL 30	On Lok Tsuen, Fanling	Ind/Godown	25,941	18.5		713
27-Nov-87	TMTL 296	Castle Peak Road, Tuen Mun	Residential	207,744	275.0		1,324
27-Nov-87	STTL 281	Sha Tin Wai Road, Sha Tin	Ind/Godown	48,911	53.0		1,084
30-May-88	CWIL 103	Fung Yip Street, Chai Wan	Ind/Godown	47,485	173.0	298	3,643
30-May-88	TMTL 316	Tuen Mun Area 40	Ind/Godown	52,251	30.0	194	574
30-May-88	FSSTL 29	On Lok Tsuen, Fanling	Ind/Godown	20,039	21.0	210	1,048
13-Jul-88	CWIL 139	Ka Yip Street, Chai Wan	Ind/Godown	49,457	194.0	320	3,923
13-Jul-88	FSSTL 35	On Lok Tsuen, Fanling	Ind/Godown	12,641	16.0	248	1,266
21-Sep-88	NKIL 6037	Po On Road, Cheung Sha Wan	Non-ind/CP	22,265	142.0	563	6,378
21-Sep-88	FSSTL 49	Sheung Shui FSSTL 49	Ind/Godown	29,714	30.5	201	1,026
28-Oct-88	LOT 1209	Pak Shek Wo, Sai Kung, DD 253	Ind/Godown	72,608	41.0	753	565
28-Oct-88	TMTL 322	Close to Tuen Mun Ferry Pier	Residential	133,414	220.0	552	1,649
29-Nov-88	NKIL 6081	Tat Chee Avenue, Yau Yat Chuen	Residential	45,764	156.0	1,263	3,409
29-Nov-88	KIL 10971	Bailey Street, Hung Hom	Non-industrial	26,619	196.0	942	7,363
29-Nov-88	KTIL 713	Hoi Bun Road, Kwun Tong	Non-industrial	48,456	420.0	788	8,668
29-Nov-88	YLTL 404	Wang Yip Street West, Yuen Long	Ind/Godown	18,307	30.5	208	1,666
22-Dec-88	KIL 10972	Argyle Street, Homatin	Residential	63,412	299.0	1,428	4,715
22-Dec-88	NKIL 6052	J/O Fat Cheung St & Tung Chau St	Godown (Dang.)	50,910	218.0	451	4,282
22-Dec-88	TMTL 318	Off Lung Mun Road, Mong Hau Shek	Ind/Godown	43,201	33.0	306	764

Appendix 1 (Cont'd)

Date	Lot No.	Location	Use	Site Area (sq.f.)	Plot Ratio	Sale Price (HK$ m)	AV (HK$ psf)	Average Land Price (HK$ psf)
Government Land Auction Analysis								
25-Jan-89	IL 8643	Harbour Road, Wanchai	Non-industrial	77,852		3,350.0	2,869	43,030
25-Jan-89	YLTL 410	Leung Yip St, Tung Tau Ind. Area	Ind/Godown	18,693		35.5	238	1,899
27-Feb-89	NKIL 5974	Wang Hoi Road, Kowloon Bay	Non-industrial	44,374		450.0	906	10,141
27-Feb-89	TMTL 297	Castle Peak Rd, Tuen Mun	Residential	104,158		227.0	661	2,179
27-Feb-89	STTL 350	Lok Lam Road, Sha Tin	Residential	16,691		12.5	1,250	749
29-May-89	CWIL 138	Ka Yip St, Wing Tai Rd, Chai Wan	Ind/Godown	25,662		105.0	337	4,092
29-May-89	FSSTL 50	Sheung Shui	Ind/Godown	62,889		86.0	270	1,367
29-May-89	STTL 250	Sha Tin, Mei Wo Circuit	Residential	10,213		4.6	1,113	450
21-Jul-89	IL 8888	Garden Road	Non-industrial	92,023		2,700.0	1,956	29,341
25-Jul-89	FSSTL 52	Sheung shui, Fanling	Residential	78,927		88.0	338	1,115
25-Jul-89	TPTL 68	Yim Tin Tsai, Taipo	Residential	31,292		10.4	416	332
25-Jul-89	FSSTL 97	Sheung Shui, Fanling	Ind/Godown	32,745		35.0	214	1,069
17-Aug-89	TMTL 323	Castle Peak Bay	Residential	227,095		380.0	560	1,673
17-Aug-89	FSSTL 98	On Lok Tsuen, Sheung Shui	Ind/Godown	13,944		15.3	220	1,097
17-Aug-89	FSSTL 83	Kai Leng, Sheung Shui	Residential	83,752		35.0	523	418
11-Sep-89	NKIL 6115	Lam Lok St, Kowloon Bay	Non-industrial	67,837		370.0	565	5,454
11-Sep-89	STTL 340	On Ping Rd, Siu Lik Yuen, Sha Tin	Ind/Godown	51,396		188.0	385	3,658
11-Sep-89	FSSTL 100	On Chuen St, On Lok Tsuen, Fanling	Ind/Godown	18,380		20.6	224	1,121
25-Oct-89	NKIL 5853	Lam Hing St, Kowloon Bay	Godown	40,935		200.0	436	4,886
25-Oct-89	TPTL 103	Ting Kok Rd, Tai Po	Ind/Godown	17,416		43.0	260	2,469
25-Oct-89	FSSTL 51	Fanling	Residential	63,669		100.0	476	1,571

Date	Lot	Location	Use				
28-Nov-89	NKIL 6056	Carpenter Rd, Kowloon City	Non-ind/CP	63,734	286.0	606	4,487
28-Nov-89	TPTL 81	Off Ting Kok Rd, Tai Po	Ind/Godown	24,004	40.0	175	1,666
28-Nov-89	FSSTL 95	Sheung Shui	Ind/Godown/Cars RP	40,742	37.0	182	908
28-Dec-89	NKIL 5983	Tat Che Avenue, Yau Yat Chuen	Residential	293,857	1,065.0	1,208	3,624
28-Dec-89	STTL 357	On Muk St, Sha Tin	Godown	36,598	122.0	351	3,334
28-Dec-89	DD252 LOT 345	Tai Mong Tsai, Sai Kung	Residential	38,212	12.1	792	317
Jun/90	IL 8740	Hoi Yue St Quarry Bay	Godown	31,215	130.0	439	4,165
Jun/90	FSSTL 82	Fanling Area 29B	Residential R3	51,667	26.0	624	503
Jun/90	TMTL 346	Tuen Mun Area 2A	Residential R1	90,417	201.0	380	2,223
Aug/90	FSSTL 46	On Lok Tsuen	Ind/Godown	26,651	33.0	248	1,238
Aug/90	TMTL 345	Tuen Mun Area 2A	Residential R1	72,118	169.0	410	2,343
Sep/90	FSSTL 117	Sheung Shui Area 4B	Industrial	10,710	10.4	207	966
Sep/90	STTL 373	Sha Tin Area 11	Godown	35,521	96.0	289	2,703
Oct/90	KIL 10985	Sung On St Hung Hom	Commercial +MCP	53,507	155.0	263	2,897
Oct/90	STTL 328	Sha Tin Area 11	Godown	33,368	80.0	257	2,397
Oct/90	LOT 236	DD229 Clearwater Bay Rd	Residential R4	20,021	8.3	1,037	415
Nov/90	NKIL 6144	Yen Chow Street	Commercial +MCP	73,733	280.0	335	3,797
Nov/90	FSSTL 53	Fanling Area	Residential	136,380	256.0	569	1,877
Nov/90	STTL 378	Lower Shing Mun	Residential R3	178,681	105.0	588	588
Dec/90	CWIL 144	Sun Yip St	Industrial	25,188	104.0	270	4,129
Dec/90	STTL 372	Area 11 Sha Tin	Ind/Godown	50,590	125.0	259	2,471
Dec/90	TPTL 113	Tai Po Area 6	Residential R2	94,722	197.0	777	2,080
Dec/90	NKIL 6145	Kowloon Bay Lam Wah St	Commercial	54,702	184.0	323	3,364

Appendix 1 (Cont'd)

Date	Lot No.	Location	Use	Site Area	Plot Ratio	Sale Price	AV	Average Land Price
				(sq.f.)		(HK$ m)	(HK$ psf)	(HK$ psf)
Government Land Auction Analysis								
18-Jan-91	IL 8781	Ormsby St, Tai Hang	Non-industrial	1,725		13.2	814	7,652
18-Jan-91	TPTL 110	Ma Wo, Tai Po	Residential	130,137		280.0	652	2,152
18-Jan-91	TWTL 344	Kwok Shui Rd, Cheung Wing Rd, Tsuen Wan	Ind/Godown	161,783		147.0	278	909
11-Feb-91	FSSTL 45	On Lok Mun St, On Lok Tsuen, Fanling	Ind/Godown	27,545		37.3	271	1,354
11-Feb-91	DD 215 LOT 1104	Tui Min Hoi, Sai Kung	Ind/Godown	30,677		14.0	117	456
12-Mar-91	API IL 122	Ap Lei Chau West	Ind/Godown	48,438		60.0	130	1,239
12-Mar-91	SIL 823	Rear of 181–205 Shau Kei Wan Rd	Non-industrial	7,818		105.0	1,370	13,431
12-Mar-91	FSSTL 96	Sheung Shui Area 4B	Ind/Godown	18,934		25.0	264	1,320
12-Mar-91	TPTL 113	Ma Wo, Tai Po	Residential	93,378		200.0	892	2,142
12-Mar-91	STTL 280	Yuen Shun Circuit, Sha Tin	Non-industrial	44,132		94.0	310	2,130
26-Apr-91	TPTL III	Ma Wo, Tai Po	Residential	112,914		325.0	1,028	2,878
26-Apr-91	NKIL 6152	Lam Lok St, Kowloon Bay	Ind/Godown	21,747		131.0	609	6,024
26-Apr-91	FSSTL 93	Yip Wo St, On Lok Tsuen, Fanling	Ind/Godown	21,162		36.0	340	1,701
17-Jul-91	FSSTL 112	Fanling Area 47A	Non-industrial	145,637		1,010.0	1,301	6,935
17-Jul-91	KCTL 436	Kwai Chung	Ind/Godown	16,534		21.0	254	1,270
15-Aug-91	NKIL 6165	Off Tat Chee Ave	Residential	59,794		430.0	2,615	7,191
15-Aug-91	KIL 11005	Argyle St	Residential	61,118		460.0	2,787	7,526
18-Sep-91	IL 8823	Wyndham St	Non-industrial	845		18.0	2,029	21,302
18-Sep-91	STTL 389	Area II, On Lai St, Sha Tin	Ind/Godown	30,559		117.0	403	3,829
09-Oct-91	NKIL 6147	137 Waterloo Rd	Residential	10,132		19.5	3,206	1,925

09-Oct-91	STTL 301	Area 30A Sha Tin	Residential	229,811		1,250.0	1,813	5,439
19-Nov-91	KIL 10986	19 Homantin Hill Rd	Residential	41,904		539.0	2,858	12,863
19-Nov-91	STTL 375	Area II, On Sum St	Godown	88,480		285.5	340	3,227
17-Dec-91	KIL 11001	King's Park Rise	Residential	69,073		900.0	2,606	13,030
17-Dec-91	NKIL 6161	Off Tat Chee Ave, Area II	Residential	112,699		705.0	2,386	6,256
17-Dec-91	AIL 923	Yip Kan St, Wong Chuk Hang	Parking/Non-ind	44,907		202.0	300	4,498
15-Jan-92	KIL 10999	Cheong Wan Rd, Science Museum Rd	Non-industrial	59,578	12.0	1,250.0	1,748	20,981
15-Jan-92	AIL 422	Aberdeen Main Rd	Non-industrial	3,732	8.2	72.0	2,341	19,293
25-Feb-92	KIL 11002	Wylie Rd, Kings Park Rise	Residential	94,842	5.0	1,190.0	2,509	12,547
25-Feb-92	TMTL 353	Wing Fat Lane, Wah Fat St	Residential	81,247	3.3	405.0	1,511	4,985
25-Feb-92	TPTL 124	Mui Shu Hang Rd, Shui Wai Area 15	Residential	226,690	2.1	800.0	1,680	3,529
25-Feb-92	SKWIL 827	A Kung Ngam	Ind	22,766	9.5	94.0	435	4,129
25-Feb-92		Wang Yip St W, Tung Tau Ind Area	Ind/Godown	35,521	9.5	38.0	113	1,070
13-Mar-92	YLTL 421	Ma Tin Rd, Yuen Long	Non-ind	57,264	6.3	415.0	1,150	7,247
13-Mar-92	TPTL 123	Shui Wai, Area 15, Tai Po	Residential	213,450	2.1	900.0	2,008	4,216
13-Mar-92	STTL 394	Sha Tin Area 148	Godown	102,258	5.0	266.0	520	2,601
13-Mar-92	STTL 395	Ma Ling Path, Kau to Area 46, Sha Tin	Residential	82,883	0.4	106.0	3,197	1,279
13-Mar-92	RBL 1067	30 Severn Rd, The Peak	Residential	24,101	0.4	33.0	3,328	1,369
28-Apr-92	STTL 374	Sha Tin, Area II, On Lai St	Ind/Godown	30,882	9.5	175.0	596	5,667
28-Apr-92	APL IL 124	AP Lei Chau West	Ind/Godown	59,611	9.5	220.0	388	3,691
28-Apr-92	TPTL 115	Tai Po Area 30	Residential	265,117	1.8	930.0	1,949	3,508
18-May-92	FSSTL 99	Fanling, On Chuen St, On Lok Tsuen	Ind/Godown	5,078	5.0	8.7	341	1,703
18-May-92	TPTL 116	Tai Po, Area 30	Residential	156,509	1.6	533.0	2,142	3,406
19-Aug-92	NKIL 6175	Berwick St, Shamshuipo	Non-ind	1,227	7.3	15.0	1,675	12,225
19-Aug-92	DD4 LOT 717	Mui Wo, Lantau	Non-ind	7,976	4.3	54.0	1,574	6,770

Appendix 1 (Cont'd)

Date	Lot No.	Location	Use	Site Area	Plot Ratio	Sale Price	AV	Average Land Price
				(sq.f.)		(HK$ m)	(HK$ psf)	(HK$ psf)
Government Land Auction Analysis								
19-Aug-92	YLTL 492	Wang Yip St, Yuen Long	Ind	40,666	6.0	44.0	180	1,082
18-Sep-92	SIL 830	Sun Sing St, Shaukeiwan	Non-ind	18,137	15.0	475.0	1,745	26,190
18-Sep-92	DD 331 LOT 237	Cheung Sha, Lantau Island	Residential	9,203	0.4	4.6	1,250	500
18-Sep-92	TMTL 370	Kin On St, Tuen Mun	Ind	26,522	9.5	32.0	127	1,207
13-Oct-92	STTL 415	On Sum St, Sha Tin	Ind/Godown	87,188	5.0	280.0	642	3,211
13-Oct-92	STTL 251	Mei Wo Circuit, Sha Tin	Residential	9,515	0.4	13.6	3,569	1,429
13-Oct-92	FSSTL 80	Area 29B, Fanling	Residential	74,272	0.8	97.0	1,633	1,306
27-Nov-92	NKIL 4932	35–42 Rose St, Yau Yat Chuen	Residential	14,122	2.1	98.0	3,305	6,940
27-Nov-92	DD 4 LOT 716	Ferry Pier Rd, Mui Wo, Lantau	Non-ind	7,976	3.9	45.0	1,259	5,642
15-Dec-92	FSSTL 163	Yip Cheong St, Fanling	Ind	31,592	4.1	39.0	298	1,234
15-Dec-92	FSSTL 149	Po Shek Wu Rd, Sheung Shui	Ind	63,195	5.0	109.0	345	1,725
12-Jan-93	NKIL 6157	Shung Ling St, San Po Kong	Non-ind	33,293	10.0	705.0	2,324	21,176
12-Jan-93	KIL 11035	Cox's Rd, TST	Residential	15,016	6.8	360.0	3,525	23,974
12-Jan-93	KCTL 442	Tai Lin Pai Rd, Kwai Chung	Ind	9,860	9.5	100.0	1,067	10,142
12-Jan-93	YLTL 456 TOWN	Park Rd, Yuen Long	Residential	113,022	3.0	345.0	1,017	3,053
03-Feb-93	NKIL 6160	Lung Pook St, Diamond Hill	Residential	280,510	6.1	3,530.0	2,054	12,584
03-Feb-93	FSSTL 147	Area 30A, Sheung Shui	Ind	129,383	2.5	164.0	507	1,268

Date	Lot	Location	Type					
30-Mar-93	STTL 393	Ma On Shan, Town Centre	Non-ind	49,428	6.7	990.0	1,442	20,029
30-Mar-93	FSSTL 148	Area 30A, Sheung Shui	Ind	28,320	5.0	65.0	459	2,295
30-Mar-93	DD124 LOT 4284	Hung Shui Kui, Yuen Long	Non-ind	19,849	6.4	155.0	1,216	7,809
30-Mar-93	NKIL 6181	Tat Chee Ave, Yau Yat Chuen	Comm	222,384	6.7	2,850.0	2,269	12,816
22-Jun-93	STTL 419	On Sum St/On Lai St, Sha Tin	Ind	43,056	9.5	385.0	941	8,942
22-Jun-93	YLTL 489	Tak Yip St/Tung Tau Ind Area, Yuen Long	Godown	32,615	9.5	46.0	148	1,410
22-Jun-93	STTL 98	Kau To Shan Rd/Ma Ling Path, Sha Tin	Residential	164,904	0.6	505.0	5,077	3,062
09-Jul-93	YLTL 486	Town Park Rd South, Yuen Long	Residential	111,084	3.0	600.0	1,800	5,401
09-Jul-93	TMTL 368	Area 10B, Tuen Mun	Non-ind	29,956	6.4	266.0	1,383	8,880
13-Oct-93	STTL 420	Area 11, On Sum St, Shatinon-industrial	Ind/Godown	45,209	9.5	395.0	919	8,737
13-Oct-93	YLTL 494	Tak Yip St, Yuen Long	Ind/Godown	38,266	8.0	50.0	163	1,307
29-Nov-93	YLTL 419	Ma Tin Rd, Yuen Long	Residential	46,823	3.0	297.0	2,114	6,343
29-Nov-93	DD4 LOT 723	Mui Wo Lantau Island	Non-ind	9,042	2.0	18.0	995	1,991
15-Dec-93	NKIL 5924	Lung Ping Rd, Kln	Residential	468,449	1.6	3,940.0	5,415	8,411
15-Dec-93	LOT 661	Peng Chau	Non-ind	20,936	4.1	82.0	955	3,917
15-Dec-93	DD 215 LOT 1107	Tui Min Hoi, Sai Kung	Ind/Godown	18,094	3.5	32.0	505	1,769
31-Jan-94	APIL 125	Ap Lei Chau, Aberdeen	Ind/Godown	61,959	9.5	4.2	705	67
31-Jan-94	TMTL 379	Tuen Mun	Godown	40,947	5.3	76.0	354	1,856
01-Mar-94	KIL 11044	Farm Rd/Ma Tau Wai Rd	Residential	75,983	5.3	2,260.0	5,599	29,743
01-Mar-94	TPTL 137	Tai Po	Residential	199,026	2.4	2,140.0	4,480	10,752
01-Mar-94	TMTL 263	Tuen Mun	Residential	84,788	3.3	650.0	2,323	7,666
31-Mar-94	IL 8688	665 Kings Rd, North Point	Non-ind	28,643	15.0	2,200.0	5,121	76,808
31-Mar-94	TMTL 380	Area 11, Tuen Mun	Non-ind	40,699	10.6	850.0	1,974	20,885

Appendix 1 (Cont'd)

Government Land Auction Analysis

Date	Lot No.	Location	Use	Site Area (sq.f.)	Plot Ratio	Sale Price (HK$ m)	AV (HK$ psf)	Average Land Price (HK$ psf)
31-Mar-94	STTL 422	On Yiu St, Sha Tin	Ind/Godown	70,127	5.0	650.0	1,854	9,269
26-May-94		Fanling	Comm/Res	223,680	5.1	2,040.0	1,774	9,120
26-May-94		Fung Kam St, Yuen Long	Comm/Res	63,390	5.9	510.0	1,354	8,045
26-Jul-94	TPTL 138	Area 2, Tai Po Kau	Non-ind	22,755	6.5	335.0	2,233	14,722
26-Jul-94	TPTL 119	Area 30, Tai Po	Residential	25,618	8.0	890.0	4,342	34,741
23-Aug-94	TPTL 136	Area 7, Tai Po	Residential	164,151	1.7	950.0	3,498	5,787
23-Aug-94	KCTL 435	Kwai Fuk Rd, Kwai Chung	Godown	36,059	9.5	220.0	642	6,101
22-Nov-94	SKWIL 811	351–361 Shau Kei Wan Rd	Non-ind	4,886	15.0	190.0	2,603	38,887
22-Nov-94	NKIL 6208	212 Lai Chi Kok Rd	Residential	898	5.4	14.0	2,887	15,590
22-Nov-94	TPTL 139	Area 2, Tai Po	Non-ind	25,478	6.4	372.0	2,274	14,601
14-Dec-94	YLTL 462	Town Park Rd North, Yuen Long NT	Residential	90,498	3.0			
14-Dec-94	KCTL 437	Area 26, Kwai Chung NT	Godown	67,189	9.5	170.0	266	2,530
25-Jan-95	IL 129	Ap Lei Chau	Ind/Godown	180,512	5.7	230.0	134	1,274
25-Jan-95	SSTL 127	Area 19, Sha Tin	Non-ind	121,418	5.7			0
25-Jan-95	STTL 108	Area 46, Sha Tin	Residential	69,966	0.4	171.0	4,073	2,444
22-Feb-95	NKIL 6204	Kowloon Bay	Ind/Godown	20,333	12.0			0
22-Feb-95	STTL 147	Sha Tin, N.T.	Non-ind	69,966	5.0			0
22-Feb-95	STTL 412	Sha Tin, N.T.	Godown/I/O	63,507	5.0			0
22-Feb-95	IL 74	Stanley	Residential	2,269	4.0	53.5	5,939	23,579

Date	Lot	Location	Usage					
22-Feb-95	KIL 11064 9	Cox's Road, T.S.T.	Residential	44,412	5.0	1,021.0	4,600	22,989
14-Mar-95	NKIL 6217	Kowloon	Residential	150,685	4.6	1,610.0	2,287	10,685
14-Mar-95	NKIL 5927	Kowloon Bay	Ind/Office	135,518	2.0			0
14-Mar-95	NKIL 6195	Kowloon	Comm/Car Park	44,175	12.0			0
14-Mar-95	TMTL 391	Area 16, Tuen Mun, N.T.	Comm/Car Park	53,723	9.5	137.0	268	2,550
14-Mar-95	STTL 435	Area 90B, Ma On Shan, Sha Tin, N.T.	Residential	117,328	5.0	1,240.0	2,114	10,569
30-Mar-95	STTL 433	Area 11, Sha Tin	Ind/Office	103,334	5.0			0
30-Mar-95	323	Sha Ha, Sai Kung	Residential	9,687	0.6	30.0	5,162	3,097
30-Mar-95	YLTL 450	Town Park Road, North Yuen Long	Residential	175,463	3.0	465.0	883	2,650
30-Mar-95	KIL 11063	King's Park Rise, Kowloon Rd, T.S.T.	Residential	168,392	1.4	980.0	1,330	5,820
28-Jun-95	SKWIL 825	Shau Kei Wan Main Road East	Non-ind	13,953	8.2	320.0	2,790	22,934
28-Jun-95	TPTL 117	Area 30, Lo Fai Road, Tai Po, N.T.	Residential	283,201	0.8	500.0	2,207	1,766
26-Sep-95	TPTL 97	Area 37, Tai Po, N.T.	Residential	164,689	0.8	280.0	2,125	1,700
26-Sep-95	KCTL 452	Shing Yiu Street, Kwai Chung, N.T.	Ind/Godown	70,235	7.5	88.0	167	1,253
27-Nov-95	TWTL 377	Wo Tik Street	Non-ind	6,155	9.5	95.0	1,625	15,435
27-Nov-95	RBL 1119	26 Mt. Kellet Road	Residential	20,832	0.6	107	8,025	5,136
19-Dec-95	IL 8870	Stubbs Road	Residential	32,764	5.0	860	5,250	26,248
19-Dec-95	IL 8871	Jardines Crescent	Non-ind	5,918	15.0	191.0	2,152	32,274
18-Mar-96	TPTL 141	Area 2, Tai Po Kau Hui	Non-ind	5,012	5.7	70.0	2,459	13,966
18-Mar-96	KIL 11084	Hunghom Reclamation	Non-ind	162,185	9.1	4,725	3,201	29,133
18-Mar-96	IL 8828	Arbuthnot Road, Wyndham Street	Non-ind	17,055	15.0	765	2,990	44,856
18-Mar-96	CWIL 156	Chai Wan Road	Non-ind	17,116	8.7	440	2,951	25,707
14-Aug-96	TPTL 118	Area 30, Lo Fai Road	Residential	228,112	0.8	525	2,932	2,345
14-Aug-96	SOIL 96	Shek O, Headland	Residential	2,970	0.8	17.0	7,632	5,724
13-Nov-96	DD4 729	Lantau Island, Mui Wo	Non-ind	7,747	2.0	10.0	645	1,291
13-Nov-96	YLTL 491	Ma Tin Road	Non-ind	45,257	5.5	370	1,486	8,176

Appendix 2

The Joint Declaration on the Future of Hong Kong between the United Kingdom and the People's Republic of China

ANNEX III
LAND LEASES

The Government of the United Kingdom and the Government of the People's Republic of China have agreed that, with effect from the entry into force of the Joint Declaration, land leases in Hong Kong and other related matters shall be dealt with in accordance with the following provisions:

1. All leases of land granted or decided upon before the entry into force of the Joint Declaration and those granted thereafter in accordance with paragraph 2 or 3 of this Annex, and which extend beyond 30 June 1997, and all rights in relation to such leases shall continue to be recognized and protected under the law of the Hong Kong Special Administrative Region.

2. All leases of land granted by the British Hong Kong Government not containing a right of renewal that expire before 30 June 1997, except short term tenancies and leases for special purposes, may be extended if the lessee so wishes for a period expiring not later than 30 June 2047 without payment of an additional premium. An annual rent shall be charged from the date of extension equivalent to 3 per cent of the rateable value of the property at that date, adjusted in step with any changes in the rateable value thereafter. In the case of old schedule lots, village lots, small houses and similar rural holdings,

where the property was on 30 June 1984 held by, or, in the case of small houses granted after that date, the property is granted to, a person descended through the male line from a person who was in 1898 a resident of an established village in Hong Kong, the rent shall remain unchanged so long as the property is held by that person or by one of his lawful successors in the male line. Where leases of land not having, a right of renewal expire after 30 June 1997, they shall be dealt with in accordance with the relevant land laws and policies of the Hong Kong Special Administrative Region.

3. From the entry into force of the Joint Declaration until 30 June 1997, new leases of land may be granted by the British Hong Kong Government for terms expiring not later than 30 June 2047. Such leases shall be granted at a premium and nominal rental until 30 June 1997, after which date they shall not require payment of an additional premium but an annual rent equivalent to 3 per cent of the rateable value of the property at that date, adjusted in step with changes in the rateable value thereafter, shall be charged.

4. The total amount of new land to be granted under paragraph 3 of this Annex shall be limited to 50 hectares a year (excluding land to be granted to the Hong Kong Housing Authority for public rental housing,) from the entry into force of the Joint Declaration until 30 June 1997.

5. Modifications of the conditions specified in leases granted by the British Hong Kong Government may continue to be granted before 1 July 1997 at a premium equivalent to the difference between the value of the land under the previous conditions and its value under the modified conditions.

6. From the entry into force of the Joint Declaration until 30 June 1997, premium income obtained by the British Hong Kong Government from land transactions shall, after deduction of the average cost of land production, be shared equally between the British Hong Kong

Government and the future Hong Kong Special Administrative Region Government. All the income obtained by the British Hong Kong Government, including the amount of the above mentioned deduction, shall be put into the Capital Works Reserve Fund for the financing of land development and public works in Hong Kong. The Hong Kong Special Administrative Region Government's share of the premium income shall be deposited in banks incorporated in Hong Kong and shall not be drawn on except for the financing, of land development and public works in Hong Kong in accordance with the provisions of paragraph 7(d) of this Annex.

7. A Land Commission shall be established in Hong Kong immediately upon the entry into force of the Joint Declaration. The Land Commission shall be composed of an equal number of officials designated respectively by the Government of the United Kingdom and the Government of the People's Republic of China together with necessary supporting staff. The officials of the two sides shall be responsible to their respective Governments. The Land Commission shall be dissolved on 30 June 1997.

The terms of reference of the Land Commission shall be:

(a) to conduct consultations on the implementation of this Annex;

(b) to monitor observance of the limit specified in paragraph 4 of this Annex, the amount of land granted to the Hong Kong Housing Authority for public rental housing, and the division and use of premium income referred to in paragraph 6 of this Annex;

(c) to consider and decide on proposals from the British Hong Kong Government for increasing the limit referred to in paragraph 4 of this Annex;

(d) to examine proposals for drawing on the Hong Kong Special Administrative Region Government's share of premium income referred to in paragraph 6 of this Annex and to make recommendations to the Chinese side for decision.

Matters on which there is disagreement in the Land

Commission shall be referred to the Government of the United Kingdom and the Government of the People's Republic of China for decision.

8. Specific details regarding the establishment of the Land Commission shall be finalized separately by the two sides through consultations.

References

Abraham-Frois, Gilbert and Berrebi, Edmund (1979). *Theory of Value, Prices and Accumulation* (M. P. Kregel-Javaux Trans.). Cambridge: Cambridge University Press.

Akerson, Charles B. (1984). *Capitalization Theory and Techniques.* Chicago: American Institute of Real Estate Appraisers.

Albritton, Harold D. (1982). *Controversies in Real Property Valuation: A Commentary.* Chicago: American Institute of Real Estate Appraisers.

Alonso, William (1964). *Location and Land Use: Toward A General Theory of Land Rent.* Cambridge: Harvard University Press.

Amachree, Sokeiprim M. O. (1988). *Investment Appraisal in Developing Countries.* Hants, England: Avebury.

Bachman, David (1990). "China and Privatization." In Ezra N. Suleiman and John Waterbury (Eds.), *Political Economy of Public Sector Reform and Privatization.* Oxford: Westview Press.

Baum, Andrew and Crosby, Neil (1988). *Property Investment Appraisal.* London: Routledge.

Baum, Andrew and Mackmin, David (1989). *The Income Approach to Property Valuation.* London: Routledge.

Berry, William D. (1993). *Understanding Regression Assumptions.* Newbury Park, CA: Sage Publications.

Bertaud, Alain and Renaud, Bertrand (1992). *Cities Without Land Markets.* World Bank Discussion Paper No. 227. Washington D.C.: World Bank.

Bottum, M. S. (1993). "Discounted Cash Flow Analyses: Tests of Reasonableness." *The Appraisal Journal,* January: 138–43.

Bowcock, P. (1986). *Valuation Tables.* Department of Land Management and Development, University of Reading.

Boykin, James H. and Ring, Alfred A. (1993). *The Valuation of Real Estate* (4th Ed.). England, N.J.: Regents/Prentice Hall.

Brabant, Jozef M. van (1987). *Regional Price Formation in Eastern Europe: Theory and Practice of Trade Pricing.* Dordrecht: Kluwer Academic Publisher.

Brown, Gerald R. (1991). *Property Investment and the Capital Markets.* London: E & FN Spon.

Butler, Diane (1990). *Advanced Valuation.* London: Macmillan.

Capozza, D. R. and Helsley, R. W. (1989). "The Fundamentals of Land Prices and Urban Growth." *Journal of Urban Economics*, 26: 295–306.

Capozza, D. R. and Schwann, G. M. (1989). "The Asset Approach to Price Urban Land: Empirical Evidence." *AREUEA Journal*, 17 (2): 161–74.

Capozza, Dennis R. (1989), "The Asset Approach to Pricing Urban Land: Empirical Evidence." *AREUEA Journal*, 17: 161–75.

Chau, K. W. , Li, L. H. and J. Webb (1996). "Past and Future Sources of Commercial Real Estate Returns in Hong Kong," under review by *Journal of Real Estate Research* U.S.A.

Corcoran, P. J. (1987). "Explaining the Commercial Reaal Estate Marker." *The Journal of Portfolio Management.* 13 (13): 15–21.

Crosby, N. (1985). "The Application of Equated Yield and Real Value Approaches to the Market Valuation of Commercial Property Investment." Unpublished thesis for the degree Ph.D., University of Reading.

Curry, Steve (1990). "Evolution of Project Analysis in China." *Project Appraisal*, 5: 2–11.

Darlow, Clive (1988). *Valuation and Development Appraisal* (2nd Ed.). London: Estates Gazette.

Diamond, D. B. (1980). "The Relationship between Amentities and Urban Land Prices." *Land Economics*, 56 (1): 21–32.

DiPasquale, D. and Wheaton, W. C. (1992). "The Market for Real Estate Assets and Space: A Conceptual Framework." *AREUEA Journal*, 20 (1): 181–97.

DiPasquale, D. and Wheaton, W. C. (1994). "Housing Market Dynamics and the Future of Housing Prices." *Journal of Urban Economics*, 35: 1–27.

Dowall, D. E. (1993). "Establishing Urban Land Markets in the People's Republic of China." *American Planning Journal*,

Spring: 182–92.

Draper, D. W. and Findaly, M. Chapman (1982). "Capital Asset Pricing and Real Estate Valuation." *AREUEA Journal*, 10: 184–200.

Edwards, Michael and Lovatt, David (1980). *Understanding Urban Land Values: A Review*. London: Social Science Research Council.

Evans, A. (1988a). "The Theory of Land Value — A Reintroduction." Discussion Papers in Urban and Regional Economics, Series C, 1 (34), Department of Economics, University of Reading.

Evans, A. (1988b). "On Absolute Rent." Discussion Papers in Urban and Regional Economics, Series C, 1 (36), Department of Economics, University of Reading.

Evans, A. W. (1983). "The Determination of the Price of Land." *Urban Studies*, 20: 119–29.

Fraser, W. D. (1984). *Principles of Property Investment and Pricing*. Basingstoke: Macmillan.

Geltner, D. (1989). "On the Use of the Financial Option Price Model to Value and Explain Vacant Urban Land." *AREUEA Journal*, 17 (2): 142–58.

George, Henry (1898). *The Science of Political Economy*. London: Kegan Paul, Trench Trubner & Co.

Greer, Gaylon E. and Farrell, Michael D. (1988). *Investment Analysis for Real Estate Decisions*. Chicago, Ill.: Longman Financial Services Publishing.

Gribbons, J. E. (1982). *Appraising in Changing Economy*. Chicago: American Institue of Real Estate Appraisers of the National Association of Realtors.

Grover, Richard (Ed.) (1989). *Land and Property Development: New Directions*. London: E. & F. N. Spon.

Han, Chien et al. (1992). *Analysts of the Changes in Urban Land Prices in Taiwan*. National Science Committee, Taiwan.

Hargitay, Stephen E. and Yu, Shi-Ming (1993). *Property Investment Decisions: A Quantitative Approach*. London: E and FN Spon.

Harvey, David (1989). *The Urban Experience*. Baltimore: John Hopkins University Press.

Healey, Patsy and Nabarro, Rupert (Eds.) (1990). *Land and Property Development in a Changing Context*. Aldershot, Hants,

England: Gower.

Ishihara, Kyoichi (1993). *China's Conversion to a Market Economy*. Tokyo: Institute of Developing Economies.

Jud, G. D. (1980). "The Effects of Zoning on Single-Family Residential Property Values: Charlotte, North Carolina." *Land Economics*, 56 (2): 142–54.

Keith, T. J. (1991). "Applying Discounted Cash Flow Analyses to Land in Transition." *The Appraisal Journal*, October: 458–70.

Li, Ling Hin (1995). "The Official Land Value Appraisal System under the Land Use Rights Reforms in China." *The Appraisal Journal*, 58 (1): 102–10.

Li, Ling Hin (1996). *Privatization of Urban Land in Shanghai*. Hong Kong: Hong Kong University Press.

Lichtenstein, Peter M. (1983). *An Introduction to Post-Keynesian and Marxian Theories of Value and Price*. Armonk, N.Y.: Sharpe.

Lichtenstein, Peter M. (1991). *China at Brink: The Political Economy of Reform and Retrenchment in the Post-Mao Era*. New York: Praeger.

Liu, H. Y. and Li, L. H. (1994). "Investment Analysis in Real Estate Development in the PRC." *Architectural Journal* (Beijing), 2: 24–27. (In Chinese).

Macleary, A. R. and Nanthakumaran, N. (Eds.) (1988). *Property Investment Theory*. London: E. & F.N. Spon.

Needham, B. (1981). "A Neo-Classical Supply-Based Approach to Land Prices." *Urban Studies*, 18 (1): 91–104.

Needham, B. (1992). "A Theory of Land Prices When Land is Supplied Publicly: The Case of the Netherlands." *Urban Studies*, 29 (5): 669–86.

O'Keefe, J. A. B. (1974). *The Legal Concept and Principles of Land Value*. Wellington, N.Z.: Butterworth.

Raper, C. F. (1976), "Internal Rate of Return — Handle with Care." *The Appraisal Journal*. July.

Ratcliff, Richard U. (1961). *Real Estate Analysis*. New York: McGraw-Hill.

Ratcliff, Richard U. (1974). *The Legal Concept and Principles of Land Value*. Wellington: Butterworth.

Rayner, Michael (1988). *Asset Valuation*. Basingstoke: Macmillan.

Ricardo, David (1963). *The Principles of Political Economy and Taxation*. Homewood, Ill.: Irwin.

Roberts, Philip J. (1975). *Valuation of Development Land in Hong Kong.* Hong Kong: Hong Kong University Press.

Seldin, Maury and Boykin, James H. (Eds.) (1990). *Real Estate Analyses.* Chicago, Ill.: American Society of Real Estate Counselors.

Sheppard, Eric and Barnes, Trevor J. (1990). *The Capitalist Space Economy.* London: Unwin Hyman.

Sinden, John A. and Worrel, Albert C. (1979). *Unpriced Values: Decisions without Market Prices.* New York: Wiley-Interscience Publication.

American Institute of Real Estate Appraisers. *The Appraisal of Real Estate* (10th Ed.). (1992). Chicago: Appraisers Institute.

Turner, David M. (1977). *An Approach to Land Values.* Berkhamstead: Geographical Publications.

Vernor, James D. (Ed.) (1988). *Readings in Market Research for Real Estate: A Collection of Previoulsy Published Articles.* Chicago, Ill.: American Institute of Real Estate Appraisers.

Walker, A., Chan, K. W. and Lai, W. C. L. (1995). *Hong Kong in China: Real Estate in the Economy.* Hong Kong: Brooke Hillier Parker.

Walker, Anthony and Li, Ling Hin (1994). "Land Use Rights Reform and the Real Estate Market in China." *Journal of Real Estate Literature,* 2: 199–211.

Wood, E. (1972). "Property Investment — A Real Value Approach." Unpublished thesis for the degree Ph.D., University of Reading.

World Bank (1993). *China: Urban Land Management in an Emerging Market Economy.* World Bank country study, 0253–2123. Washington D.C.: World Bank.

Yeates, M. H. (1965). "Some Factors Affecting the Spatial Distribution of Chicago Land Values, 1910–60." *Economic Geography,* 41: 57–70.

Index